## Acknowledgments

*For the few who stood by me while the many judged, bullied, turned away and shunned. Carolyn, Neil, Peter, Mary, Sydney, Doug, Dave & Julie, Sadie & Keith.*

*For all who have had to suffer indignity, bullying and prejudice.*

*For my brothers and sisters in North Korea who are under persecution daily because of their faith in Jesus Christ.*

*Thank you to:*

*Mo Pimenta for proof reading my story and having faith in me.*

*Mr. Fear (English tutor 1981 – 1984) for introducing me to "Mark Twain". Sir the seed was planted it just took a while to grow!*

*Also, thank you to Alison for helping me to get back my dignity.*

*Special note:*

*Hey Moorlands I actually did this with totally no Star Trek quotes! I guess miracles do happen!*

*In memory of my Grandmother Joan (Nana) who sadly died of cancer in early 2009. I am sorry that I never got to explain everything to you.*

## *Special note*

*As you read this book please take note that names, dates & places have been changed to protect peoples I.D, privacy and without being too dramatic, for some their lives. I pray and hope that this will not reflect on what has been written and that you, the reader, will understand.*

*Many thanks in advance.*

*Jason*

*If you have questions or you feel effected by this book please email johneleven43@yahoo.com for a response and further information.*

Copyright 2010 Jason K de-Vaux Balbirnie

Cover design by Jason K de-Vaux Balbirnie

Book design by Jason K de-Vaux Balbirnie

All rights reserved

ISBN 978-1-4461-6789-2

No part of this book may be reproduced other than by prior agreement by the author

The only exception is for a reviewer, who may use short quotes in review

Printed in the United Kingdom

First printing August 2010

# Prologue

It's freezing, not just cold but truly bitter. It hasn't been this cold since the winter of 1976 or so the weather forecast would have it. Standing on the platform I muse at the glittering frost twinkling on the concrete looking strangely beautiful in the early morning sun. The station feels almost asleep as though it doesn't want to have to wake and would prefer to stay in a blissful stasis until spring. A few early commuters are hunting for a hot drink grumbling about the cold weather although you would think this should be expected after all as it is December. The speaker just above my head crackles into life announcing that my train to Cambridge will be on time which is a relief as so many trains have been delayed because of the ice and snow. I have little time for a margin on this trip what with someone collecting me on arrival that has been pre-arranged to get me to the interview on time.

The train pulls into Cambridge station, on time! The journey was uneventful other than snow clad trees and fields. As I walk out of the station I scan the area looking for a car with a friendly face, a face never seen as we have only ever talked via email. Having told my contact to look out for a tall bald guy looking lost I see a driver in a car across the way, he looks a little like a cavalier, I put my hand up in a kind of greeting which is met by a similar response and pray that as I approach the car this is not one of these less than comical misunderstandings. It's ok the cavalier is my lift, we actually find it all a little amusing, this guy checking out all the bald men coming out of the station, he says he got some funny looks which is not surprising. The humour of the moment relaxes us as we drive into the city.

Wesley Methodist is nothing like its pictures on the internet. It looks older than its ninety eight years, not in a gothic or falling apart way but well preserved. I can't but help feel its friendly disposition on arrival taking me back twenty odd years to another church that felt similar.

The day is rigorous, possibly the longest interview I have ever experienced culminating with a panel of four people asking questions like bullets from a Gatling gun. I feel like a contestant in front of Lord Alan Sugars "The Apprentice." By 4pm it's all over, it has been a six hour epic and I'm feeling exhausted. I head back to the station on foot letting the cold air clear my mind; I get lost on the way and find myself in a park where Christmas is in full swing boasting an ice skating rink with groups of happily chatting people and some very excited children. The light is fading quickly and as dusk falls the festive lights adorning the park stretch the silhouettes of the crowds shadow giving everything around me almost a Dickensian feel. I allow myself to enjoy the scene for a few moments before getting on with finding the rail station. By the time I eventually get to the platform there is a twenty five minute delay, there is nothing anyone can do when this happens, and all you can do is wait. My mind can't help but wonder how many times over the years have I found myself waiting on one platform or another. Oddly to say but it feels like half my life...................................................

# Short accounts of the imperfect Christian

**In the beginning: Bubble gum and lolly sticks.**

**My first experience of church was not the most conventional and most certainly not a road to Damascus conversion.**

**At the supposed innocent age of thirteen I was caught red handed stealing from the offertory boxes of the ancient Anglican Church that adorned the middle of the village where I then lived. To say it was just me would not be true, however here I was, the one who had been caught and therefore would have to take the consequence of action, anyway my so called mates had since denounced me to be the ring leader and shunned me as if I were a leper.**

**My father was one of stern military like discipline and when he heard of my crime naturally went ballistic caning my hands until they bled while explaining to me that I was lucky because in some Arabic countries they cut thieves hands off – needless to say I didn't feel very lucky. I was then frog marched down the road by the scruff of my neck to the vicarage. My meeting with the Rector, and this**

confused me as he wasn't called a Vicar, was looking back a God send as he turned out to be a really nice jolly kind of chap who saw my discretion as quite an adventure and applauded my ingenuity of lifting coins out the offertory boxes using Bazooka Joe bubble gum and ice lolly sticks. Sadly my Father was not so forgiving and thought it a great punishment if I was to become a altar boy and the new church bell ringer – suddenly God to me wasn't this nice guy who sat on a cloud with a beard cooler than ZZ Top, instead he was this punishing old miser who certainly liked to punish and had no sense of humour! So my penance began and I and God started a love hate relationship. The lesson I learnt that day – "Next time I won't be caught!" And true to form I wasn't until a week before my nineteenth birthday.

I spent the next six years of life running wild and being a law unto myself. By day at school teachers saw me as a scrawny kid who could be an angel but when out of sound and mind of adults lurked a creature inept in deception and dishonesty. The older I became the larger the creature grew within me.

**The Mission on the green**

We moved as a family from the village to a local market town and this larger space became the playground to a host of pranks and stupid behaviour on my part as my attitude rapidly went downhill.

Now at the age of seventeen I had a real attitude and contempt for anything considered an authority and a hatred of any religion, church, Christian or God. I was a teenager with all the usual hang ups and hormones a perchance to dress in the then style of the new wave movement and the ability to get what I wanted by being a charmer.

One particular day walking down the road looking in various shops at my reflection (did I mention I was vain)? Thinking "I'm looking good today", I had a piece of paper pushed into my hand by a very smiley looking person and my heckles rose due to the writing on the said piece of paper "TENT MISSION". I was about to throw this offence back at the person who still looked all teeth and nothing more in my opinion, followed with what would have been some not thought out rude remark when I found myself grinning and saying thank you - as I walked away I was laughing, I had a plan.

That evening with friends in tow we walked across a playing field and into what looked like a big top. We smiled (and quietly sniggered) through all the songs and listened to the talk given by the friendly looking minister. At the end we even said thank you and shook hands. An hour or so when all had gone home we returned and cut all the guy ropes and threw a good few tent pegs into the near hedge. Thinking we had managed the perfect crime we left laughing finding the whole episode hilarious. What I hadn't counted on was the consequence of action that would follow me to four years in the future.

**All bad things must come to an end**

Having left school a year before the mission tent incident I was having the time of my life. I had managed, and I don't know how, to get into the local college on a pre-nursing course which suited me fine as it was more practical than academic with a bonus that the course was 99% girls. Having finished college I started working for the local health authority – I was obviously still up to my shenanigans but in a weird way I had a code of honour, while at college and then work I was involved with the care of mostly vulnerable people and I realised deep down that these people needed help and it was not their fault that I had decided those few years back to walk the path I was now on. Looking back I feel it fair to say, yes there was obviously a part of me that showed good intent, but then again back then as soon as I was out of what I saw my "public official" situation I was bad to the bone.

By now I had graduated from petty theft and minor chaos to an accomplished grifter who had a side line of hot wiring ignitions and picking door locks. I was running with a gang, not your stereo type leather jacket thugs but suited and booted with neat haircuts that gave the appearance of well mannered polite and educated young people, let's be honest it was the eighties and which teenager didn't want to dress to kill and be a poser? Regardless how good you can look you can never dress up your reputation and under the smart suits and would be style, mine was very tarnished indeed. I was also caught up within the romance of the situation in an alternative world seeing myself and then friends as modern day folk heroes, the Robin Hood's of the eighties with the style and demur of the great fictional thief Raffles. We would strut the streets as peacocks in love with ourselves and what we thought we had achieved, oh we thought we were so great and that everyone loved us, bullet proof and indestructible. I would say I was afraid of nothing and I readily took on stupid and dangerous challenges and then one day the unthinkable happened and all I thought I knew suddenly changed.

There I was minding my own business, posing, drinking a cup of coffee with a Moore's cigarette held between my second and third finger trying in the entire world to look cool with a purpose. The sun was shining and it was a pleasant early May and I remember revelling in the warmth with the feeling of smugness that I daily lived with. I was meeting up with a friend, not one of my usual then friends but a guy I worked with, a nurse who I found ok to get on with which was unusual in itself as I never really moved in any other circles but that of the group I ran around with let alone a male nurse. However, I said I would meet at the coffee shop I frequented and after all it was still early in the day and most of those I usually socialised with would not be up and about to well after mid day. Seeing my friend coming I took a final puff of my very fashionable cigarette and ordered more coffee.

We small talked for about half an hour and I could tell this man in front of me clearly enjoying the day as I, had something he wanted to say. In the end I guess he must have felt my frustration with our idle chit chat on the weather, work and upcoming summer so he finally said that he knew I would be insulted and angry with what he had to say, inside my head I could hear myself saying just B........ get on with it, my perception of the world around me started to slow down and I no longer felt like a hunter but the hunted, I was trying to smile and nod to the words I was hearing but inside I was tensing up as though I was about to enter a ring and fight for my life.

"God wants you to know that He loves you," he said. Well, all was good so far, I hadn't jumped up from my chair and attempted to re-arranged my friends teeth with my fist "God knows you're afraid, but Jason, God wants to use you" Ok enough was enough, whether my friend was delusional or not I wasn't scared of anything, which I told my friend and added that if God was speaking I felt it a little rude and tell me these things now and not a few years ago when I really needed to hear them. By now the sweat was trickling down my back and it was not the heat of the sun, my heart was racing and I was desperately looking for an exit while keeping my image I projected intact. My friend sensed this and he could have easily pursued his advantage but he didn't. Instead he apologised if I felt he had been rude and started to organise himself to leave. Relieved and thinking I had managed to successfully blagg the way I was feeling I relaxed. My friend, about to walk away suddenly turned to say what I thought would be a cheery goodbye and then my world rocked unsteadily as he asked, "So are you saying you are not afraid of anything?" " Not anything" was my reply. "Ok", he said cheerfully with a smile," See you Sunday evening at Church then." This was obviously not a rhetorical question but a challenge. He walked away and I felt sick, the day no longer felt so good anymore, and was that a black cloud peeping over that distant tree line?

The challenge was set and for the first time in quite a while I found myself looking for an excuse not to go. I could say just shove it and laugh it off, but then again what if it got out I would never live it down, besides all I had to do was sit in a pew for forty five minutes or was that an hour? Anyhow I convinced myself that I could brass it out. I had met my friend on a Tuesday and waiting for Sunday to come was like extracting teeth, not that I was in a hurry to get there but the want to just get on with it. The other weird thing was in the days leading up to my meeting with church or as I decided to call it "The Church Challenge" I found myself not being able to enjoy my usual nocturnal activities, I couldn't bring myself to enjoy the chaos that I usually got so excited about to the point that those I was with offered to take me to the local hospital A & E.

Sunday finally arrived, worse still I awoke early having tossed and turned all night dreaming vividly of being the thirteen year old me, my hand trapped in an offertory box while my father kept repeatedly saying "Thieves have their hands cut off and the Rector smiling at me saying "It's ok you can be an altar boy and ring the church bell"!

I spent most of the day in my rented lodgings trying to work out a last minute plan and living in hope that my friend was ill or just couldn't make it. I was trying to run away from the future because somehow I knew that my future was about to catch up with me like the last day of school or college when you realise you are no longer a child or student and you have to face the real world that is adulthood.

At 5.45pm I started to walk to the Church to meet my friend and fate, it didn't take that long to walk the distance but I took the long route with the notion that I might meet with someone who would need me to help them or some other such excuse that I could give later in apology to my non appearance. No such luck! There at the end of the road stood the church looking very Anglican and old, could this be history repeating itself in some strange way? As I neared I could see the huge oak door that was then the main entrance and my friend waiting for me with some other church looking people, all looking curiously happy with pleased and bizarrely welcoming faces. Putting up my hand in a kind of wave in greeting to the waiting group at the door I took a deep breath that was to be my last in the outside of the world as I knew it.

What struck me first as I entered through the door was that old musty, yet aromatic smell I guess is the residue from the use of pungent incense? The church was fairly well lit, loads of stain glass windows and wooden pews, YUK how I hate wooden pews! Even to this day I tried to avoid them at all costs, a Christian curse that tries even those with the strongest posture and always without exception leaves you numb bummed with the accompaniment of pins and needles when you eventually get to stand up and walk again.

I shuffled into the furthest back pew I could find, the nearer the back the better was my thought, good for a swift exit when it all got too much. Sadly the pew started to fill from either end with yet more happily faced people, this crowd were fast turning into a dentist's nightmare. It was then it dawned on me I was trapped as I suddenly found myself in the middle of at least 4 people either side, funny that as the pew didn't seem that long when I first crawled into it no more than five minutes ago. Trying to get myself as comfortable with no hope of escape I inwardly groaned as the music started with my friend being one of the musicians looking so happy with his flute I thought he was going to burst.

After the songs, there were at least five, groan, and some prayers, more groans, then what I thought would be the talky bit, "well this is a surprise", thinks I, as a teenager who looked all of fifteen nervously walked to the front coughed politely and started to talk. It wasn't the most engaging of talks I had heard and after a few moments having said he loved Jesus he sat down, "thank God for that" I said under my breath, let's get on with the sermon before I lose all feeling in my bum and then another teenager approached the front, then another and so on until I had heard at least twelve stories of how they had all met Jesus, all different yet all with the same ending being "I became a Christian."

By now I had lost my indifference to what was said, in fact it all was suddenly engaging and I was feeling dirty and uncomfortable, not in the I have ran a marathon and really need a shower dirty but a sense of disgust with myself that I had never felt, a realisation that I could actually be wrong and had been blaming God and the church for who and what I had become using them as a scape goat to justify the way I lived my life. A big hole was now opening in front of me and I wished it would just swallow me whole, I was still looking for an escape but now the tables in some bizarre way had turned as I realised how wrong I was, all I wanted to do was run, impossible the grinning crowd either side of me had bowed their heads in prayer and I felt suddenly exposed and alone.

The rest of the service was a blur, a dark moment in my history where I sat as a statue only aware of my heart thumping and the blood rushing in my ears like the ocean crashing on rocks and the words going round my head that Jesus was alive, He offered forgiveness and He had died for everyone – did that include me? And then coming to my senses I realised the service had ended, people were standing and chatting and someone ask "are you ok"?

Looking up I saw my friend just beaming another of those smiles that I had frequently seen since arriving. Clearly he could see that I was distressed and invited me to his house for coffee with a couple of his friends I had met earlier that evening on arrival. Wanting out as soon as possible I almost ran out of the church with relief gulping the fresh air that greeted me greedily as though I was a drowning man fighting for his last breath.

# The thief on the cross part 2

I sat on a chair hugging a hot drink trying to analyze what had transpired in the last two hours. I was shaking, having walked into a church as a God hating criminal to a man who so unsure what he believed or thought anymore. The room was full of conversation not just about the service we had all sat through but ordinary stuff of which when spoken to I nodded and weakly smiled at, really could they not tell I wasn't interested as I was having a life crisis. It's just a little hard to discuss your favourite TV programme or what washing powder you use when you have not long come to the realisation that all you believed in or knew was in fact nothing but a pile of steaming pooh! I'm unsure who started what happened next, I think it had to be me as I remember stating how dirty I felt which was followed by someone making a poor joke that there was a shower in the bathroom. NO! I shouted I am dirty, my insides, my thoughts, my life, everything is disgusting. The room's atmosphere seemed to change like the static you can feel just before a storm breaks over your head. My friend asked simply do you believe in God Jason. My answer...Yes but he doesn't want someone like me, I'm no good, a fraud, liar and a thief, why would the Almighty want to choose someone like me. There was a moments silence as I looked worriedly around room, in the background played a cassette of some singer I had never heard of singing El Shaddai, El Shaddai, and in one of life's odd moments, just when I was at a point of confusion all I could think was "What the heck does El Shaddai mean"?

My friend spoke to me through the mist, or was this tears that had formed around me, "If I can show you in the bible right now someone like you who God forgave would you pray to Him and ask for your life to change?" Ok I said, did I really say that? All of a sudden I had the urge to leave, to get back into the world I knew, away from the guilt I had been feeling for the last couple of hours – I wanted to run and hide. My friend read from the end of the gospel of Luke (Luke 23: 39 – 41) where Jesus is crucified between two criminals, one mocks Christ saying if you are the Christ save yourself, while the other asks Christ to remember him, Christ even at the point of His own death forgives the criminal and says, "From this day you will be in paradise with me" and that was it! The one sentence that brought me knowledge of a new life, I was that criminal and I wanted to believe. I prayed, my heart broke and the change started, not all at once you understand but a seed had been planted and I knew this seed would grow.

We can all make empty promises for tomorrow, what Christ offers is salvation today. If we are in a place where we feel all is wrong in our lives and we need God and then pray for Christ to enter our heart and nothing happens, then truthfully what Christ promises can't be true and therefore why not just carry on the way we are knowing there is nothing in the end but death and emptiness, however if we do pray honestly with an open heart for Christ to come into our life and we change, then surely have we not gained everything?

I awoke the next morning, it was a beautiful mid May outside, the sky was blue and the birds were singing, for the first time in my life I awoke to myself singing in my heart, I realised something new had happened and I felt the excitement not unlike that of a child who wakes on Christmas morning to a barrow full of presents at the end of their bed. The change had started and the euphoric feeling within stayed for at least three months, and I still mourn to this day it going away, over the past few years I have again felt a similar sensation and all I can conclude is that in my opinion it is just a tip of the teaspoon taste of what Heaven will feel like. I have many times tried to evaluate why this heavenly feeling comes and goes, My conclusion is that unfortunately we are all imperfect, tainted by this world and all the sin around us, as Christians we are continually moving towards perfection when we meet our Lord either by His return or when we shed this mortal coil and I surmise that as we discard our worldly baggage, trauma, guilt, hate etc we have moments of grace given us, possibly God's way of showing us through His spirit that we are not alone as we continue to change into Christ's image. From the moment we ask Christ into our lives we are at war with sin and it is not long before our attention can be taken from trying to walk as a Christian to that of the world, affairs and problems of life. Thus begins the battle of the spirit.

**Chronicles of early events**

**The would be musician:**

It was not long into becoming a Christian when I started to discover the musician within me. I had tried to involve myself in playing with a band before, although it always ended up as an excuse to get blindly drunk and do a "WHO" impersonation smashing up your instruments.

I had played the keyboard for a few years, as a hobby really, but saying this though who can't admit they haven't stood in the mirror at one time in their life and mimed air guitar to their favourite track? I was now nineteen years old and very much into the new wave scene, you could say I became obsessed with the idea of writing modern Christian songs/hymns and with two friends from Church went to a recording studio in Norfolk to cut a record from the two songs I had recently written. I convinced myself that God was in this, and anyway wasn't music in my blood? I have some family connections in the music business a 60's/70's producer the now late Edwin Astley, who was my great uncle by marriage and Pete Townsend of the "Who" who was my great aunty and uncles son in law. Before going to the studio I had written to Uncle Edwin who had commended my song writing ability and on the strength of this alone I was flying high and in every way thought I was to succeed and take God out into the world amongst the many teenage fans who would surely come to listen. Everything just went to my head.

We named ourselves "His Word" and five thousand singles were printed, we got on a local radio programme and all seemed right and exciting. It never ceases to amaze me how easily we can get distracted from the path we intend to walk. Yes, looking back it was all fun, no we didn't make any money or have hundreds of adoring fans, thank God someone, I think it was then my youth group leader, had it in them to point out that God was possibly not calling me into a life of witnessing to a fan base and the rich and famous. Realising that what was happening to me was destructive I started to put on the brakes. I'm unsure if God hands out consolation prizes? However what did happen was when I realised what an idiot I was, I recorded another track in York with a non Christian friend. This record did ok in the European club scene, sadly never to be heard of in the U.K, but this did encourage me to continue with writing worship songs. To this day every now and then I will blow the dust off my guitar and lead worship or teach a new song – the keyboard now lives at the end of my desk in the office, I still love the sound it makes and from time to time it comes out and makes a cameo appearance.

I sometimes look back and think "What if" (great name for a band if you want to use it)! I realise had I continued with the music path that I would have failed; had I not, knowing who I am today I can safely say it would have destroyed me. When dreaming remember, all that glitters is not gold! In our Christian walk we have to make some tough decisions as we travel through this life, this was one of them. It's amazing that what can seem so beautiful is actually very deadly and destructive.

## Hypospadias

Being ill is never fun. At one point I decided that I wouldn't add this chapter and then recently having talked to a friend of twenty years whose wife is chronically ill in hospital it came to my attention that I should.

I was born in 1968 with a congenital defect known as Hypospadias. If you want look it up on Google but to explain exactly what it is would take pages upon pages of your reading time. Bottom line it's a malformation of the urethra that needs correcting. Sadly in 1968 I guess medicine isn't advanced as it is now. I went through a good part of my early life with a fair bit of surgical procedure causing strictures that cause pain and put pressure on my kidneys. My school years were dominated with embarrassment as I often had little to no bladder control. Because of my condition I was no good at sports and my confidence levels were below zero. Without doubt some of the hate I felt toward God as a child evolved from my confusion and agony as I tried to bargain with the Almighty and try to get to grips with why it is me who had to suffer. It wasn't until many years later having become a Christian that I realised it was never the

Lord punishing me or singling me out because I was destined to do some great evil. Unfortunately the world in which we live is a fallen one and much we see hear or suffer from is a direct consequence of this. It's no –one's fault that I was born with this condition, it just happened and in the greater view of things I can count myself blessed as there are far worse things that befall many people in this life.

God is good in all things. Through my own physical suffering I have come to a place where I can sympathise and empathise with those who daily suffer in various degrees of illness. I am blessed man; it is far harder to praise God for your sufferings than to complain and call down curses because of your situation. Because of what is wrong inside me I have had the privilege and opportunity to witness to many hospital staff and fellow sufferers. Christ carried a cross for me so why should I complain? The apostle Paul talked of his sufferings and it is now obvious to me that no matter if we can see peoples ailments or not we all suffer in some way within this life. Truthfully I can say to you that my pain is bearable knowing that Christ is with me, why He chooses not to heal me in this life I don't know, but I know that one day my Father will call me home and my suffering will be no more, in the meantime: "PRAISE THE LORD"

# The calling

So we become a Christian, what happens next? Normally and naturally we go to church on Sundays and during the week inevitably get involved in whatever programme the church / denomination puts on i.e. prayer meetings, youth group, meals and the like. This is all great stuff and to begin with as a new Christian very enjoyable, I loved the social aspect and getting to know people and myself, however after a year I felt more and more uncomfortable with what felt like ground hog day. Please don't get me wrong Church and all involved in it were great, and still are, it was a feeling like an expectancy, a time when your toes first touch the blocks before a race begins I felt a desire, a thirst that needed to be quenched, to learn and experience more, and this was a sudden knowledge that there was more of God out in the world. It was a drumbeat in my heart and when I sat for prolonged periods to think about how I was feeling my heart would miss a beat and a nausea that was both sweet and sour. Going to an elder in church and explaining was difficult but needed, the answer I received was at first not what I wanted to hear – "pray and seek God" Being a young man of now twenty years I could be stubborn and arrogant, traits of many young men, however after a few days of feeling I was beyond this praying thing I came to the realisation it was the only way forward, so pray I did.

Having prayed for a week or more and at the point of giving up I got an answer to prayer. A group of us would go to the larger town six miles down the road on a Saturday and hang out with a Christian Youth organisation that would go out and street evangelise amongst the throng of weekend shoppers. It was here I first experienced sketch board and street theatre, crafts that I still use in ministry today. It was here within this then fledgling youth movement that I realised my prayers had started to be answered. I gleaned and took in everything I could, became more confident and studied the scriptures. Then one particular day a friend of mine told me he had put in an application to a London based organization for a year in evangelism. This is it, thought I, knowing that the moment was right. I approached my church and youth leaders who given the time I had been a Christian were very encouraging and supported me in my application. It all seemed to happen so fast, I gave notice with my then job in residential care and the days flew by. On the night before leaving I had dinner with my youth group leaders, it was an emotional time and I felt a little sad to be leaving, a great deal had happened to me in eighteen months and I questioned myself as to the certainty of the direction I felt pulled towards. One of my youth leaders took me to one side and put my mind to rest. He was very wise, as I believe him to be today. At the end of our chat his final words at that moment in time have always stayed with me. "It's great you have felt God's call and you are leaving to follow it, however remember once you leave you can't come back." This was a little shocking at the time, especially that he had taken twenty minutes to assure me that I was doing the right thing and I found myself contemplating this particular sentence for a fair few hours. It wasn't until many weeks later when I returned did it dawn on me what he was saying. Having gone about three months I returned for a visit to discover all had changed, time had not stood still and indeed the church, people, town etc had moved on without me, it was only then I could fully appreciated that God had moved me on, but in doing so I had to leave the past behind as I stepped into a new chapter of my journey.

So here I was sitting on a train hurtling toward London, my entire life's possessions now stored in a rucksack and a small sports bag between my knees. I watched as the scenery outside flashed by and gradually changed from country scene's to the high top of offices and flats of the city, I had arrived in London.

London Bridge station - May 1989.

It was filthy, hot and VERY noisy, people pushed past me as though I didn't exist, and if they had seen me they just didn't care. I was not totally green to London but my past visits had been with a huge bunch of friends to go clubbing or a coach trip to Wembley to see a band play at the stadium. This was totally different, scary yet brilliant at the same time like a moth that can't but fly towards a flame knowing that it could get burnt – or worse. Here I was strolling down the street in the hub of the capital feeling every inch the wandering evangelist, a sense of belonging, a feeling of euphoria, I had made it, just one problem to deal with then – I'm lost!

I had been off the train no more than ten minutes and already I'm lost, I looked blankly at the map the Mission has kindly sent me realising it was useless as I struggled past yet another group of tourist who for some reason wanted me to walk in the gutter and under a bus. The info I had recently received in the post failed to mention all the commotion and hub bub. As I desperately looked around for a street sign or land mark I couldn't help but sarcastically think that perhaps this was the real entry test, if you get to the mission headquarters you're in, if not go home? Then just as I was thinking all was hopeless and I should re-trace my steps I saw a beautiful apparition appear on the horizon, an angel if you will a metropolitan police officer. Having explained my predicament she kindly led me along Tooley Street to London Bridge Road where she left me gawping at the building in front of me, London City Mission headquarters. A few minutes later and a lift ride later I sat with bags outside the youth director's office, you would have thought I would have been here before for interview but back in the day it was all letters and references. My first meeting with the Youth Secretary was very brief, a pleasantry about my arrival and was the map sent easy to read, I started to speak and was going to explain about my encounter with the police officer but given the situation felt it was inappropriate. His next comment was a shocker, you need a haircut! In 1987 I sported very long hair which had grown from an 80's mullet, looking at me now you would never believe this as I have more resemblance to a cue ball than a wild rock band type, but in the day blah, blah, blah. It needs to be above your collar was his next remark, oh yes and a tie for church events. Looking back it could have been worse but then the comments bit into me, I hadn't prepared myself for this, didn't Jesus sport long hair? And come to think of it, I don't remember reading anywhere that he wore a tie. Thanking the youth secretary for the opportunity he had given me I left his office and headed towards the stairs. I had been instructed to follow the stairs to the bottom where I would find the rest of the team cooking and doing something called SPAN packing, I thought I had misheard and felt too embarrassed to ask if I had, surely he meant spam, I mean they were cooking lunch right? I arrived at a double set of doors and heard talking and laughing in the room beyond. I opened the doors to fifteen pairs of eyes looking as I walked in, backpack over shoulder, my Fedora hat pushed casually to the back of my head, trying to look cool and confident. I strolled over to a nearby table and looked around at my team mates; someone said "Welcome to V.E" This was going to be interesting!

A motley yet interesting bunch stood in front of, all casually dressed, all stuffing envelopes with a glossy looking magazine. After a few introductions and brief chit chat came the question, "so you're here to help do the SPAN"? It was then that it became clear that SPAN, and not SPAM was the magazine being stuffed into envelopes. So this was to be my baptism of fire and not standing on the corner of a street yelling out a message from the bible? Everyone else, turns out it was a great team building exercise, by the time we finished and ate lunch, which incidentally was not spam I felt I had been part of the team from their inception the previous September.

## Kings Cross

Awaking the first morning I was a little stiff, possibly too much SPAN packing, I wondered if I was to again be asked to make my way back up to H.Q for another round of monotonous enveloping. Having arrived quite late in the evening to the base, where we all lived as a team, I barely had the chance to take in my surroundings which were basically a hostel that used to
be an old Victorian medical mission, built on two floors with a cellar, which I am sure once served as a mortuary, which was a kitchen, dining and drying room.  After breakfast there was a meeting in the lounge, a room that had seen far better days with

Winnie the Pooh painted here there and everywhere, sofa's that had came out of the ark and an old 1970's record player/stereo in the corner.

The base was run by house parents who led the meeting and then announced that I would be joining the team at Kings Cross, so no SPAN packing then? Great! My head was now buzzing, I had money put into my hand for a travel warrant, a few seconds to nod to my new found team and we were off.

London, a place of adventure, excitement, museums and galleries. A place where the United Kingdom is governed and draws thousands of tourists every year. Then there is London, a place of misadventure, prostitution, homelessness and drugs and this London I was about to meet and get to know.

Kings Cross Mission hall was like most an old Victorian buildings, no surprise there, it stood not far from the main station and underground, the area around it was filthy with litter and rubbish everywhere. Down the road prostitutes touted their business and every so often, in fact often a car would pull up with the occupants selling powder and pills. In what seemed every doorway sat a bag of bones with hollow eyes, hand outstretched trying to catch your eye, hoping you would offer some coin that would no doubt be helping to fund the next can of Special Brew. A shock to the system, my dark past had been centred on idyllic little rural towns and villages with twee shops and it struck me how, as bad as my life had been how easy I had it. I spent the next three months working amongst those in need while the majority of the general public would simply walk by putting blinkers on themselves from the reality that was normally under their feet. The word of God was powerful on the street's and although most days felt dark and depressing and at times scary you could see how the Spirit of the Lord worked amongst the lost and broken hearted setting people free. Nothing had prepared me for this work but this was not a bad thing as in those early months I learnt how to think on my feet and be prepared for all eventualities.

Many things happened that I witnessed while with the Mission in Kings Cross, however two accounts have stayed with me these last twenty years and will no doubt always stay fresh in my mind probably due to how these two situations changed me more directly to everything else that happened over that time period. Although I had read in the bible that we are not in a battle that is physical of flesh and bone, but as Christians, from the moment we are saved we are in a spiritual battle with the powers of darkness, for me it had only been words that described a situation. Through the two accounts I would like to share with you and became fully aware of the spiritual realm with whom we co-exist as followers of Christ.

Having been at the Mission hall for a while my missionary in charge said to me one morning that he had received a phone call from an Australian man who was in need of real help and asked would I accompany him to meet this man at a one of the many walk - in clinics that can be found dotted around

Soho. Truthfully I was unsure due to being given the choice, which had not happened before and feeling my missioners tension as he was asking me, then again on the flip side it felt like an adventure and experience I shouldn't miss.

On arrival at the clinic we were met by the Australian, who on first glance came across as a man in peril who was down on his luck having come back to the U.K from living abroad. I then noticed that we were in a psychiatric clinic and the hairs on the back of my head stood on end as the person talking to my missioner Cleary was a nurse and telling us just to leave the man as "He was cooking" and "could possibly be dangerous" My missioner didn't feel that dumping this man was an option and with that headed into London in our van, me in the back with our new friend, who I became aware was no longer talking in the same accent, in fact his whole personality had changed. My stomach started to turn as our friend went through several personalities as we drove for about twenty minutes and it dawned on me that the man we had with us had some serious problems.

So here I was sitting in the back of a clapped out mission van, the doors are locked and my missionary had gone off to find some help. We were in fact at a psychiatric hospital, my missionary knew our multi persona friend would no doubt jump out in fear or one of his nastier persona's could suddenly erupt and hurt someone, so thinking for the best he had left me in charge in a locked van. Our friend was by now climbing the walls, or is that van sides? One moment we were talking calmly about Church, God and Jesus, the next he became aggressive trying to punch his way out of the van windows. All I could do was to pray, and so I did loud and clear, I believe God stepped in because I am still alive today to tell the tale. Thankfully the cavalry arrived in the shape of my missioner and two burly looking gentlemen who were more like contestants from Mr. Universe than psychiatric nurses. Our friend was admitted for the night and I thought, well that was the end of this adventure – wrong, the next day we returned, my missioner had organised a prayer meeting at a church for our friend. So again we all got in the rickety van and hurtled down the road a few miles to an old Gothic looking Anglican Church. On arrival we were met but half a dozen others it was explained that it was possible that our friend had been manifesting demons, hence his multiple personalities. Now this was all new to me and truthfully I felt quite scared. I waited outside, peeking through the door every so often and quickly walking away as loud cries and shouts echoed through the old church cloisters. This went on for half an hour or more and then all went very quiet. My friend emerged a while later looking pale but smiling, my missionary told me all would be well and we drove back to the hospital and delivered our guest back to two more Mr. Universe nurses. The last I heard was our friend had moved on having dealt with his problem. For all I know he might have been given the right medication, but I believe after seeing and experiencing all that poor man went through that God met him at his point of need and he was able to move on with his life. Today I believe there are people with mental illness from life crisis and problems. I also believe there are many people out there in bondage to more than mental illness. Both are relevant, both need prayer, love and support, both need Jesus Christ as their Lord and Saviour.

A month or so later there was another phone call. Again I was asked if I would like to accompany my missioner on a mission of mercy. By now I was a little more aware of how this missionary worked and although it usually meant the unusual I was always keen to jump aboard for the experience.

We made our way to an estate. Having parked outside a small terraced house I was filled in with the details of why we were here. We had come to see a single mother who had phoned the mission in distress over furniture moving around her eighteen month old daughter's room, on its own, no strings attached, and the feeling that she was not alone, bottom line she felt haunted by a poltergeist. Having prayed we entered the house. All seemed quiet, not anything like I expected having watched the film Ghostbusters too many times. We went into each room and prayed and all was still. The lady kindly went to make us some tea. We were chatting casually when out of nowhere a cupboard started to move, not a wobble as sometimes happens due to uneven floor or from the vibration of traffic, no this cupboard went for a walk a least a couple of feet. With that my missionary prayed with the mother and for the daughter and for Christ's peace to fall upon the house and loudly told whatever it was that was doing these things to leave. The prayer finished the house fell into a different kind of silence, a peace that passes all understanding. Yes, you could argue that what I was feeling that day was in my imagination; however there were two other witnesses to the events written and they felt this peace too. Our battles as Christians are indeed not of this world, but against the legions of darkness that prey on those who live in fear of dark corners, who attack through our weaknesses, who set out to destroy people's faith and belief. We left that house that day knowing that God had done a work there and this woman would not be troubled by this event again. We left with words of encouragement and my prayer is that from what she witnessed she would hook up with a church and seek salvation from Christ.

I have had many other experiences of which some I am sure to write of later. However these situations and events changed my way of thinking from being a two dimensional to a three dimensional Christian, it challenged all I had learnt so far in my young Christian walk and gave me a new thinking towards what is seen as spiritual and reality.

Now having served six months as a voluntary evangelist with City Mission we came to a two month break. I was given the option to come back for another year at the end of the summer of 1989 which I readily accepted and on my return having worked in Austria as a team leader for O.M's Love Europe, I progressed to what was known as V.E 2, basically a second year for those returning. I sadly said goodbye to my placement in Kings Cross where I had learnt and gleaned so much and which I am still grateful for today. I was then moved from the base in Bermondsey with three others to a flat in Earlsfield where we were to become designated the mobile unit.

A year on the move

Four individuals, four backgrounds, four very different personalities, another clapped out van and a new missionary in charge, this was going to be interesting and a time when I first became aware of the phrase "Heavenly sandpaper." We were quite a mix although we already kind of knew each other from V.E 1 we had all worked in different teams and locations so other than small talk and the odd grunt over breakfast I would say we hardly knew each other at all. This soon came to light as our living together became frustrating and agitating. Who would wash up? Who didn't clean the bath after use? Who knows how to use the washing machine? Who missed the toilet? Things you would normally take for granted if you live at home were suddenly magnified and blown out of all proportion. Yes we had all lived communally together at Bermondsey but even that was governed by house parents. Here we were four young men having to learn domestication together for the first time. It really had its moments but respectively it did help us to gel as a team. If anything it personally taught me patience and that my way is not always the right way.

For the first couple of months we trained on the job which was a no guts no glory education, jumping out our van at various locations setting up and delivering sketch board messages, which is basically painting with words using the Gospel as your message, and then jumping back into the van to repeat the process at another location. Twice a week we had a break from our hit and run evangelism by spending time at the a West End soup kitchen, feeding, clothing and sharing the Gospel with London's homeless population. Then on weekends we went to various churches that the mission supported where we would either actively share in the service or support our missioner as he preached. It was a truly mad year full of challenges, humour and most importantly witnessing the works of God upon the City of London. It was never easy and there were times I am sure all four of us wanted to just walk away. Such was this year and the bonding of friends that to this day I am still in contact with two of the team, the third sadly we have all lost contact with, and my then missionary. Through the frustrations, successes and failures of my experience with London City Mission I learnt and grew so much. I still use my experiences of then as part of my ministry now. They truly were days of glory and I feel privileged that I had the opportunity to share in them.

In 1989 Billy Graham came to London and the mobile unit were part of the stewarding team. During the main talk a homeless man was sitting at the front of the seating area where we had been stationed. It was noticed that there was at least three chair spaces either side of this man who had his head down and was sobbing. Our missionary walked down to where this poor wretch sat and asked "Why are you crying?" The man replied that he had heard about the love of Christ, but then if this is true why were all the Christians sitting away from him? Our missionary looked at everyone sitting in the nearby seats and asked why no-one wanted to be seated next to this man? Eventually there was an embarrassed reply that the man reeked of filth and old alcohol. He was indeed not looking great. His clothes were practically falling off and torn, his shoes had holes, his beard was tangled and matted and from head to foot were stains and sores caused by goodness knows what. On hearing the reply to his question my missionary put his arms around the man and hugged him. My point, all Gods children need to be shown love.

## Bible College

While serving with the mission I got accepted at Moorlands Bible College. My year at the L.C.M had been a real testing ground for my calling. A few months into the Mobile Unit I got offered an interview at the college. It was autumn and as I walked up the lane into the college grounds the leaves were falling off the trees. It was an overnight affair and the next morning having experienced a night of Moorlands student hospitality I was ready for my interview.

I arrived at the principal's office five minutes early and nervously checked my shoes and flies (don't ask). Invited in to take a seat it was announced that there would be another member of staff involved in the interview process and he was on his way, small talk was made for a moment or so and then the other half of the interview duo came through the door. Standing up to shake hands this man said to me directly without a word of welcome or introduction "I know who you are" Well that was obvious; after all he has surely seen my application. I felt eyes burning into me and felt worried, yet curious. Would this be a trick question? I replied." No" came the reply," cast your mind back a few years to a tent mission which you visited",  suddenly I was feeling nauseous, "It was MY tent mission, and YOU smashed it up." This man before me was the then Baptist minister of the town where I grew up. He went on to tell me that I had been seen with others cutting the mission tents guy ropes." I'm sunk", went through my head, I won't be going to Bible College then!

I sat in silence not sure what to say, how cruel is my fate, to have been pulled out from the fire of Hell itself, to have moved on and feel the Lord call me, to be serving Christ in London and now everything was about to go down the pan because of a past action that I had long since forgotten. By now my mind was whirring and I fought back the temptation to try and concoct some excuse or half truth that might get me out of this huge black hole I was so suddenly in. My panic started to turn to anger at myself cursing the day I robbed that village Church all those years ago, the pathway it had led me on to this humiliating finale, my punishment complete? Out of the blue and quite unexpected there was laughter, were they laughing at my unfortunate set of circumstances? No, they were smiling and commenting on how far they felt God had brought me in so little time. My heart started to slow, a trickle of sweat ran down my spine and the interview continued to conclusion. As I was leaving the man, the ex Baptist minister whose Mission I set out to destroy said "I made some calls this morning. There were a number of people I just had to ring and tell them, you will never guess who has walked through the college gates today"!

I heard about a week later – I had been accepted into Moorlands Bible College. Many times in my life to date I have experienced situations of uncertainty and surprise but nothing has ever come near to that day at interview when God showed so clearly that He had a path for me to follow and that particular autumn morning having received my acceptance letter I revelled and basked in what the Lord had done.

It was a sad day when I said goodbye to the London City Mission. It had been eighteen months of adventure, learning and growth. To make matters sadder I decided to leave early so I could spend the summer making money to help towards my college fees. It was a hard summer as I broke my back on a building site as a brickies labourer, which if seen must have been pretty comical as I was all of about twelve stone and was more a rake than muscle bound, following the builder up ladders to supply him with what felt like a never ending supply of materials. As it turned out at the end of the summer my home church very generously paid for my first years fees and I received a full bursary for year two. So here I was again standing at the train station with my life packed into two bags. It was late September 1990 and as I stood on the platform gold and red leaves were dancing in the breeze around me. The season was about to change.

## The Bible College years

College was a mad time, I arrived thinking my next two years would be of reading profound theological books and learning all the answers, or at least to have all the gaps filled. Actually my pre conceived idea of what would happen was completely wrong. Yes there was a lot of study to do, and papers to write but there was also a sense of freedom, to be able to explore who you were as a person as well as a Christian.

As much as I was happy at college in my first year I struggled academically. And at the end of the first year I failed which meant harder study and catch up in the second year. I spent the summer of 1991 fretting about returning and constantly questioning if going back would be the right thing. My tutor had also moved onto pastures new, the new guy whom I had already met seemed ok and so I decided not to judge this man but to try and get to know him as it would be key to my success and eventual graduation. It became clear that I had to get a grip of myself, stop panicking and change my attitude.

The second year seemed to fly by and as time moved on my work improved and as it did so my confidence grew, new horizons for the future started to appear which further challenged and stretched to seek God's will in my life while learning to recognise my weaknesses as much as my strengths.

July 4$^{th}$ 1992 will remain in my memory as a momentous occasion, the day I graduated from Moorlands. Independence Day indeed. The weather was perfect and it was a great valedictory service. To add to these happy events was the further good news that I had been accepted for a third year and that I had been offered the funding to do this. Life was great and before me was a smooth road with success written on it. Nothing could have made my life more perfect at that moment of accomplishment – Oh yes; did I forget to mention I had fallen in love?

Toward the end of my second year at college I had met someone while on mission at a local Baptist Church. Since L.C.M I had decided not to get romantically involved with anyone partly due to my only serious relationship prior to college had broken up and partly because of my lack of academic prowess that always needed my attention. Nearing the end of my last term and realising things would turn out well I felt myself relax for the first time in a while and while on mission it just kind of happened – as it does!

When you're in love you tend to do irrational things that you wouldn't normally consider, you walk on air in between the universes of reality and never never land, everything feels great and if anyone says to you, you are making a mistake, regardless who they are, friend or not, let's be honest you are not likely to listen, I am no different and as my brain turned to mush a spiral started to turn that would eventually destroy me, hey but what did I care? I was in love.

**Good decisions, Ok decisions, bad decision**

Now looking back at myself after my graduation I inwardly cringe. My life could have so easily been so different, yet my common sense seemed to have left me. Everything I had worked for, all my dreams, all that the Lord had done for me I threw away. You see I was now getting married and I no longer needed further training after all I had worked in London, I had a great testimony and I was going into ministry. Cleary I had lost the plot; it was all about me an arrogant young stupid fool – truthfully at this point it's fair to say I hadn't learnt anything other than to pander to my own desire and want.

I turned down my third year, got married and went to work for a Church as their Youth Minister.

It was hard graft. The Church was part of an Anglican team ministry situated on a large council estate that had obviously seen far better years. Working with most people was great, they had a heart of gold but like most built up area's in modern society it had its trouble spots. On a Friday and Saturday night I worked with a small team of volunteers trying to do something with the youth who were naturally hanging around the streets in boredom with nothing but crime, alcohol and drugs to entertain them. We started to run a club called "The Rave at the Knave" which proved quite successful, so much so the local rag did a story based on my past and the work I was now doing. This led to another job on two larger estates and I lived in the belief that I had made it. The church was seeing a lot of youth work and the community appeared to be benefiting. By now I was pastoring several groups of young people, doing chaplaincy with the local cadet units, Royal Marine family's and my work at the church seemed to double over night when the Curate in charge house caught fire and while repairs were being made he and his family moved a distance from the church which entailed giving me more responsibility. I was now working eighty to a hundred hours a week oblivious to what is was doing to my marriage and health. Again a good friend tried to point out that I was heading into trouble, again in arrogance I failed to listen. Inevitably something had to give and tragically my marriage collapsed. It wouldn't be right to start apportioning blame to everything that happened in a crazy ten months; I can only take responsibility for my part. It was a difficult time. I left the church not because I had to but because it was the right thing to do, if you're not firing on all twelve cylinders it guarantees that you will make serious mistakes and when working with young people or old your behaviour and decisions can have disastrous consequences on their lives.

I went to work for a housing organisation hoping to find myself and start repairing my damaged marital situation, this was not to be as things got worse and people took sides, there was rumour and gossip as friends became enemies. Very few stayed neutral and it wasn't long before there seemed to be more enemies than friends. Exhausted and fed up my faith started to backslide at such a phenomenal rate that within a couple of months I no longer recognised myself. Looking in the mirror one day I realised I had degenerated back into the excuse of a human being I would have been years before if it hadn't been that I had met Christ. My heart hardened and I became critical of church and sarcastic about its practices. Those who I loved turned me away at the door leading me to sink lower and then worse still when two churches sat down with myself and then estranged wife and practically brokered our divorce. It was a time of destruction, finger pointing, lies and tall stories, but there was still more to come.

Being alone in the world is no fun. You walk past people alive with laughter, shouting and getting on with their lives; you walk past as a ghost, the world around you in slow motion. Just going to the corner shop exhausts you as all you want is to sleep and never have to deal with what's real anymore. Time seemed to stand still as everything that has happened plays on a continual loop around your head. You are that person who is in the crowd yet alone. I shut my mind to God, Jesus, Church and friends. I didn't hate them it was just that I could no longer bear the pain of talking or praying about everything that had happened. The wounds ran deep into my very soul and had become infected. I was walking as one of the undead.

There were those who laughed and jeered who, verbally abused me, who called me liar, coward and fraud, that I was demonised with an unclean spirit and that I deserved my fate. All I wanted was a little understanding, some reassurance and having not seen the milk of human kindness from those who were then closest to me I snapped and headed straight for oblivion into a vodka bottle. I have always been a take it or leave it person when it came to alcohol but at this moment in time I just wanted to numb the pain that was constant inside me. I took a beach hut for the summer and spent the best part of three months drinking myself stupid as the days melted into one. Then one morning I simply woke up and everything seemed to have changed. The pain had gone; the heaviness that just dragged me down was no longer there. It was time to move on, time to re enter the real world. I still felt betrayed by my friends but concluded that I could get on without them and the Church just as well. What I didn't want to do was go into a life of crime and surmised whatever happened it was to be legitimate and within the law. I moved back to the town where my I first became a Christian ten years previous. I had no intention to go back to Church; it was familiar ground that I desired. Within a few months I had stabilized and was working for myself doing advertising. It wasn't perfect and more often than not the money was poor. However it was a start in the right direction and regardless of financial problems it felt good to stand on my own two feet again. Having worked for a year or so I again moved back to the south coast, this was a business idea as I was now more involved in advertising to students and the South Coast had a glut of language schools that seemed attractive.

Although initially not the smoothest of moves it wasn't long before I had established myself with the local language schools doing various deals that attracted the students and was equally profitable to myself. Within a few months the business seemed to morph into other areas such as parties and nightclub promotions. Business was good and life was a breeze, as the money rolled in the suits got more expensive and the partying went into days. With everything looking right and me feeling I was a success I started to go back to Church, just sitting at the back to start with but before long at the front leading the worship. Nothing was real, it was all about me and the persona I had created which being a thin veneer wasn't destined to last. Business was still booming and now added to my so called success was a mobile phone shop. From the outside the shell which was me looked respectable, successful and a man who was involved up to his neck with Church. The truth was a man crumbling inside who was forever plugging up problems on the damn he had built around himself, within business, personally and spiritually, conning the ego that if he could give it a few more days all could be turned around. There is only so much pressure a damaged damn can take before it breaks down causing the walls to fall. All I had done was to whitewash over and over all my problems believing that if they could no longer be seen they would eventually disappear.

Christmas 2002 was when disaster struck, mobile phones were not selling as they had and the student promotions were going sour. The money started to dry up and I found myself closing the shop and taking various jobs to try and keep my head above water. Further to my humiliation I had to move out of my home to a much smaller flat and go to work for a D.I.Y chain that crushed the life out of me. Watching wallpaper dry would have been far more life giving. Within a year I had had enough of gritting my teeth through a fake smile while some member of the public jumped up and down like a spoilt child because he couldn't find the right size packet of screws required and it was clearly the fault of whoever was serving him to know exactly where it was because they were in a hurry. One particular day I simply took off my apron, told the customer that when he eventually found what he was looking for he could "Shove it" where the sun don't shine! Feeling liberated I walked into the sunset, well not quite, more three hundred yards down the road to a company selling plastic windows and doors, within two hours I was offered the job as there telesales manager and all was well in the world for another six months.

Plastic companies are renowned for a high turnover of staff and I learnt that having the title manager just meant your neck was on the block when the company targets were not met. Having failed in my monthly target even though for five months the team I had run was successful and profitable it was my turn to become unemployed. I didn't want to go on the dole and decided to try the self employed route again. This time it was in corporate delivery, which was just a fancy name for delivery of leaflets and menu's. It was ok, not huge money but it paid the rent.

You meet a lot of interesting people in business when you deliver their leaflets, within a few weeks there were plenty of free kick backs especially from fast food owners and restaurants and it's not long before you start to socialise and build friendships. I started to move in and around circles of business that used my service and more often than not they owned local restaurants but had bigger fish to fry in areas such as import / export. In another bout of arrogance and stupidity I wanted to push ahead and try yet again to put myself on the road to success and I figured it a good plan to involve myself with importing cheap goods into the U.K. This I started to do with a couple of people who were close to me and felt I could trust and as usual all was going well. I was still attending church but my heart just wasn't in it, all I could see was pound signs and a quick fix to life's problems. You would think I would have learnt my lesson by now and realised that I was on yet another self destruct mission but there was to be no stopping me.

I always took pride in what ever business caper I got involved with was legal. Regardless of my motivation in wanting to be successful there was always a line I wouldn't cross, it got near to the knuckle a few times but whether it was my past regrets for my behaviour before I joined the church or my fear of God I always walked away from what looked like, and often was a hooky deal. One evening I met with those I was doing business with and it was put to me that a lot of money could be made in bringing people into the U.K to study and then find legitimate jobs. Because I and another had British passports we were asked if we would become sponsors of these students of which we would be paid a fee, then the conversation seemed to darken as it was put to us that there were others who would like to come to the U.K and we could also offer sponsorship to them as we had a business and could offer work, again for a fee. Unsure and listening to what was being said I just nodded and sat quietly as I felt it prudent not to commit myself and realising there was something more to this conversation. Thinking it would possibly be a better deal which was less complicated I unwisely stayed when it would have been better for me to have left at the moment as the next hour was to change my life and take me on a journey to a very dark place.

Another man entered the room and I recognised him as a businessman from Pakistan who a couple of years previously had bought a large amount of mobile phones from me when I still had the shop. We had more food and coffee and socialised with pleasantries. My business friend (who I was in business with) and I were asked how much money we would like to achieve earning and how quickly would we like to see this happen. As much as his question was engaging I felt myself take a step back inside myself, something was wrong and I started to look for the moment when I could remove myself from the conversation. It was time to go home. The man talked of his home and oppression, of men who only wanted to defend themselves, their families and homes. My business friend was sitting on the edge of his seat looking very excited and then came the part of the conversation that I had been dreading and before I could get up and leave a deal was set on the table to help export weapons to the far East via Pakistan. Numb and realising things had gone too far I started to look for my coat while the conversation continued, my friend now totally hooked. As I was leaving the small group of men I thought I had known I tried to make a joke of the whole episode telling myself that they were only testing me to see how far they could push my morals. Sadly I knew this wasn't true and that unwittingly I had been privy to something very serious. You would think that after having such a conversation that you would have gone straight to the authorities, yet another classic Jason mistake. My friend in business was close to me and I hoped that he too would walk away and I felt I should sleep on what had happened, contact my friend in the morning and then decide what should be done.

I was awoken the next morning about 5am to my mobile phone ringing, I choose to ignore it but by the third time when it started again I answered. My mind was awash with the night before and I was groggy from waking up so early and abruptly. It was my friend who was at my front door wanting to urgently talk to me. Letting him in thinking he was in trouble I made some coffee and tried to wake up. My friend looked grave and very serious, "You didn't buy into us telling you it was all a joke" nodding, all I wanted to do was go back to bed – could this not wait? "Ok truthfully what was said last night was no joke, my new business associates are concerned that you might go to the authorities", I was told, which was true, "I have convinced them otherwise, but they say unless you are on board with the deal they will have to make you disappear"! I couldn't quite grasp what was being said – disappear?
"Jason they will kill you" My head was spinning, kill me? This can't be happening, this just doesn't happen in the real world. This has to be some sick

joke. My friend looked at me with concern "I'll help you pack" he said.

On the run

When I was a child it was a fantasy of mine and many other kids at the time to be James Bond, thrown into intrigue involving plots to take over the world through acts of violence. The reality as you no doubt already know is far from the world of tuxedos, Walther PPK's and super gadgets to get you out of a tight corner. The storyline was that the good guys always won, this is not what happens in real life. Over the period of a few years my life had spiralled out of control. I had gone from Bible College graduate with a ministry to so called business man to someone who had nothing and was now about to go on the run in fear of his life. The truth is that I was already running from myself long before events got this far out of control – bottom line, I could only blame myself for the events that had led me to this place and situation I now found myself in.

Having packed everything that I could carry I gave to the keys to my friend with his promise that when this whole affair had blown over he would bring me the rest of my belongings, I was never to see any of my possessions that I left that day again. It was about 7.30am as I hurriedly made my way to the rail station, I just wanted to get as far away from what was happening as possible. The first train that arrived at the station heading toward London I was on, even though I couldn't shake the feeling that I was being followed and was relieved when on arrival at Waterloo station I could lose myself amongst the crowds of people that were standing around. I had a couple of hundred pounds on me and I holed myself up at a cheap B & B for a couple of nights while I took stock of the situation. On the first night my mobile rang. My friend told me that those involved knew I had gone into hiding and were making it general knowledge that if I went to the police they would take revenge by going after people I loved, unwisely I thought it best to stay out of sight until everything had sorted itself out, surely they would get bored of looking for me? After all in the great scheme of things I wasn't so important. With money running out fast I found my way into the surrounding countryside sleeping in hedges and barns. I came to rest for a few weeks at a horse farm where I ended up being so hungry I was eating the oats that were given to the animals. Then for a while I bummed around various parts of the U.K working cash in hand giving my name as Jamie Smith but never staying in one place for more than a few days from fear of my past catching up. Eventually I managed to settle in a small town in rural Suffolk doing small DIY jobs. I rented a room and keeping my head down tried to get on with life as best I could.

The owner of the house went to Africa for three months giving me more room and freedom that I hadn't experienced for quite a while, I was happy with my work and although still concerned about my experience of recent months it now all started to feel like a bad dream.

I awoke with a start, the phone was ringing and realising I had over slept I guessed it was a potential customer. Grabbing the phone the voice asked if he was speaking to Jason, having said yes I was expecting to engage with the usual conversation that would follow about price and the time frame the job would take, instead came the reply, "Good I am a C.I.D officer, would you mind coming to the front door as we have need to talk to you." Obviously they must have been watching the house so there would be no point lying and fobbing them off with the "I am not at home" speech. Preparing myself for the worst, but hoping for the best I went downstairs in dressing gown and having shown me I.D I let the two officers in. They could see I had just woken up and possibly due to this and them seeing the shock I must have been in they suggested I sat down. "Jason de-Vaux Balbirnie I am arresting you on suspicion of arson with intent to kill" It was all very confusing; I tried to find words that would help me – anything? But nothing came to mind. I was allowed to dress and go to the loo then taken to the local police station to the custody suite (need to say to any police reading this, PLEASE change the name of what you call your holding cells, cells are what they are and pleasant titles using the word suite should be used for posh hotels only). Having been searched I was placed in a cell and told two officers from the C.I.D on the south coast were on their way to interview me, it could be a long wait and would I like tea or coffee?

My new home for the next few hours was very spartan with a bed area and toilet, no toilet roll. Time had stopped, having searched me my watch was taken so I had no idea what time it was or how long I had been locked in my cell. Lunch came (polystyrene) with a doctor who talked to me about depression and left with the custody sergeant some lovely blue pills to take if I needed to calm down. My mind racing I started to wonder why I had been arrested for arson and not for anything to do with trafficking weapons illegally. It was all a conundrum and all I could do was await the two mysterious officers from the south coast who were now well on route to see me. After being held for six hours I was going mad, the police managing the cells were great and very generous with the tea and coffee and even found me a few magazines and a toilet roll though it wouldn't have mattered if I could have had a T.V or cinema experience as all I wanted was to see the investigating officers to get to the bottom of what was going on, I most certainly had not set fire to any building let alone tried to harm anyone.

Another two hours or so later, it could have been a shorter or longer time but without a watch time can feel very odd, the cell door opened and an inspector told me they were short staffed and I was to be moved to another station about 15 miles away. With that I was handcuffed and led to a waiting van, on my way out I was greeted by two plain clothes officers who were in fact the two I had been waiting for. Grimly I greeted these officers with "I would like to shake your hand but given that I'm handcuffed "which was met with more of a scowl than a smile. These two, I decided certainly have no sense of humour! Arriving at another police station and another custody suite, again I was put in yet another cell, handcuffed to begin with, which was smaller than my pervious abode, with graffiti of various other poor souls who for reasons bad or worse had the unhappy experience of cream walls with a green trim, small metal toilet, low ceiling, bad lighting and a very hard excuse for a bed. On a positive note my handcuffs were removed on request, I was given toilet paper, ten minutes in a what looked like a 14 x 10 yard for fresh air, a blanket, some ok coffee and the opportunity to have a solicitor, with service such as this why should one complain?

Following another epic wait the two CID officers eventually arrived and I was "invited" to the interview room, phew, thought I, at last I can sort this stupid affair out. Offered more coffee my interview began. My solicitor, found for me, was brilliant and insisted I was allowed to wash and clean myself up as best I could before we started, put in a small bathroom nearby I looked in the mirror to see a man who had aged ten years in twenty four hours, my eyes looked tired and scared and my cheeks had sunken in. Having got over the shock of how I looked I washed quickly, the water feeling cool and cleansing on my skin reviving me for the next round.

The next three hours I was grilled about an incident that had taken place about a month after I went on the run. A second hand shop who I had cashed some cheques with some months before had burnt to the ground, there was a flat next door and thankfully the occupants had got safely out. It was impossible for me to have been there to commit this terrible crime as when it had happened I had been over 250 miles away and working, this could be proved but the interviewing officers were still not convinced. A photograph was produced and I was asked if I recognised the person it. "Yes" was my answer that's my old business friend, in black and white staring at me was my friend who had told me to run, standing outside a cash machine a few doors down from the shop that had gone up in smoke on that same night. I was then told that several cheques had been cashed in my name and had bounced, most of these had been destroyed in the fire. The penny then dropped. My so called friend had obviously been using my name to bounce cheques and I presumed he was trying to cover his tracks. Although concerned that with any information I gave the police could start me on the run again I told them my theory while omitting the events that had led me away from the south coast. I panicked and was scared that if I went into everything that had happened I would be held in custody forever. All I wanted to do was to be freed and hope that I could repair any damage that had been caused by my arrest. Finished with me for the time being I was released on bail.

I took a cab back to the house. It was very late and I had been gone about eighteen hours. Walking through the door my heart sank, the house was in pieces and resembled a war zone; the police had a search warrant and had obviously forgotten to clean up the mess they had made. Starting to clean up I realised I was far too tired and flopping onto my bed strewn with clothes and cd's I fell into a deep and troubled sleep.

Morning broke and as I woke up my sleepy mind tried to work out whether I had just been through a bad dream and I would wake up with all well in the world. The shower was luke warm as the emersion had not been switched on; the tepid water helped me to wake up. Over a coffee I surveyed the mess before me, just about every draw had been emptied as had the cupboards in the obvious frantic search of evidence that had not been found as it was never there in the first place. I was grateful that the house owner would still be away for another three weeks, had she been there I was sure she would have asked me to leave there and then. The cleaning and repairs took two days and in that time my mind filled with what had happened and how this would all end. I tried to ring the man who had been my friend to try and make sense of everything only to connect to the message box. After several attempts I gave up. I was alone.

The house owner returned from Africa. I felt it best to tell her the truth what had happened. She was of course furious but before she could ask me to leave I collapsed and later found myself in the local hospital. Having been admitted for a couple of days the prognosis was that I was suffering from stress and dehydration and the next day I was released. As I was leaving the ward I was given a hand delivered note, it was the house owner telling me not to return. It was a typical autumn evening as I walk out the hospital doors, wet, cold and dark. With virtually no money I randomly picked a direction and started to walk, the direction was insignificant and I guess it always is when you find yourself homeless without hope feeling soulless.

Walking amongst the fallen

It had been a hard few weeks with little respite, my feet hurt and I was filthy. I slept as much as I could during the day in a library or any warm place I could find, but mainly libraries huddled in one corner or another with a book trying to dry out. Frequently the mind would take me back to my time in Kings Cross and those lost souls who would peep at you over a dirty rag, the hollow eyes filled with nothing but despair, and here I was feeling like I had been taken out of time. Plunged back into an alternate reality where I become one of those poor lost creatures. Hunger and cold now became my worst enemy. You get so hungry and numb that your mind starts to play tricks on you, while you go all but mad just for a slice of bread. It was a tough and monotonous life. It was nearly December and I had just about given in when I managed to secure a job working for a UPVC company. The manager took pity on me, there was an empty flat above the showroom and although against company policy he allowed me to stay there, no electricity or heating but I felt like a king after the hardship of the street. Christmas was fast looming and working hard I had managed to earn a little bit of money. About a week before Christmas day I went to bed as usual. My room was on a middle floor landing with the showroom and officers below. Above me was another old flat that had been recently closed off as the floors were unstable. It was about two in the morning when I heard the walking on floorboards in the rooms above me. To begin with I thought it to be my imagination, and then the noise got louder as whoever was up there was trying to force the door to the closed flat open. Hastily I pulled on some warm clothes and entered the hall outside my room, I could see a shadow dancing on the wall at the top of the stairs, switching on the light the hallway looked misty, then it dawned on me what the dancing shadow had been. The flat above me had been set on fire.

I made my way down the stairs and into the showroom, the smoke was now very thick and it was getting harder to breath. As I unlocked and raced out of the front door the cold hit my face like sharp needles and my lungs filled with iced air. As I went around the corner to get clear of the smoke I saw a dark figure jump the back wall, shouting I started to give chase but my body had been weakened from my recent homeless experience and it was not long before I was short of breath and near to collapse. Making my way back to the bottom of the road I dialled 999 from a call box across the street. By now the top of the building was well alight and great gusts of smoke were filling an already pitch black sky, then came the sound of screaming sirens.

The police arrived almost the same second as the fire engines. As the fire-fighters got on with their job I was invited to the local police station to make a statement, it was an attractive offer as it was bitterly cold, there was nothing to fear as I had done the right thing and I kept telling myself this as I climbed into a waiting police car.

Having given a statement and given coffee as promised I was asked to wait as there were a couple of things the officers who had done the interview wanted to check. It was now around four in the morning, going to an all night B&B seemed the right thing to do. As I was about to leave the police station I was asked if I could wait a few more minutes. The inner door opened and out came two uniformed officers followed by the words; "We are arresting you!" I could hardly believe what I was hearing and had to ask the officer to repeat what he said. Another badly painted cell with graffiti "BONG WAS ERE" and "ANDY DIDNT DO IT 2003" come to mind. Had I been cursed? I began to wonder on the odds of being arrested for arson twice within three months. They must have thought I was crazy or worse as they left the door to the cell open most of the time with a different officer on the door every two hours.

The next morning I received a visit by the local CID who explained I had been detained on suspicion of arson as I was the last person in the building and they had found no trace of the man I had seen running away. The people who had a flat next door had seen a man taking a ladder and when asked in an I.D photo if this man was me it was realised they indeed had the wrong man. I was released having been held for twenty hours. My clothes had been taken from me and sent to CSI for tests to confirm I had nothing to do with the fire. It was humiliating to say the least and when I eventually got to a backstreet B&B I cried like a baby. I was beyond scared; especially that it had been asked why anyone would want to burn down a building with me in it. Again I should have told the truth, again I was stupid but what I then realised was that I was in a lot more trouble than being suspected of arson – someone still wanted me dead.

Christmas 2004 was very cold. I had gone back to living on the street, I felt safer being anonymous. Boxing Day night was beyond freezing and I dare not fall asleep in fear of not waking up. I must have walked around for over fourteen hours until the winter sun eventually rose on the skyline. Although the air was icy its warmth seemed to sink into my chilled bones. It was still the Christmas holidays and I was unsure of what to do or where to go. There was money for a little food but not enough for a room. The pavement was slippery and it was all I could do to keep my footing walking down a hill into a town that was familiar, I had been here before. A man was walking up the hill toward me, wrapped in coat hat and scarf, we passed each other. "Hi Jason, are you ok?"

Exhaustion had got the better of me, the voice I heard seemed a long way off and my knees started to buckle. Strong hands kept me up and led me gently down the hill, into gate and through a front door. The heat hit me as though I had walked into a furnace. I was sat at a table with a hot drink and toast and slowly I started to regain some composure. Having eaten and drank as though my life depended upon it I looked up to see two smiling faces. Not angels, although that had crossed my mind as I nearly passed out, but two old dear friends. Incredibly I was seated in a room within a house I recognised, I had once rented a room here many years ago before going to

Bible College. All I could do was sob as they showed me to a room with a clean bed.

The next day over breakfast my rescuers asked me no questions. I felt I needed to explain though. I started from the beginning telling them everything, it all sounded crazy and I was sure I would be shown the door at any moment, this didn't happen. Instead I was given clean clothes and told to go back to bed. When I emerged later thinking the worse I was told a safe haven had been found for me. Within a week I again found myself on a train heading toward a community where I was told the priest in charge had a special gifting for those who were in trouble, had a life crisis or found themselves to be lost.

Arrival

The train pulled into a little station in the middle of nowhere. As the train pulled away it was just me and my bag on the platform. In the distance as the noise of the departing train faded I could hear cows moo their dissatisfaction with life as they searched for food. Taking the lane away from the station I made my way along the narrow pathway that led to a small town. Asking for directions I ended up walking down an even narrower pathway until finding some gates tucked in just off the road. An old green sign was hung next to the gates; its green paint and black lettering had seen better days as I noted how cracked and weathered it was. The gates groaned with age and lack of oil as I stepped into an entrance to what had once been an old monastery. I was met with a pleasant aroma that emanated from a bush by the front door. "Well, no going back now" I thought as I rang the doorbell. A kind and smiling face opened the door "hello, are you here for lunch?"

My welcome was not what I had expected, neither was the building, which was a hotch potch of very old architecture and what appeared to be circa 1970's style brick. The dining room was a mass of table and chairs and then a bell was rung. Various individuals appeared out of what seemed like nowhere happily chatting as they took a place at the table standing behind their chosen chair. A brief silence followed by a short prayer and everyone sat down. The food was good, practically home made everything. What I noticed was that the tables were facing each other, rather like something from the legend of King Arthur and true to form as everyone ate all seemed content and happy with their portion as if no man was above another. Lunch finished and I was invited to the community office to talk with the Priest in Charge and his wife. It was difficult to tell my story all over again, so much had happened and a lot had yet to finish. The Priest and his wife just sat and listened only asking to clarify a point when needed. I was never once shunned or judged, ridiculed or laughed at, just listened to. At the end of my story it was felt that the series of events that had concluded with my arrival may well take a while to untangle. I was taken to a room which was now mine for the duration and I wasn't sure what to expect next but what was certain was that for the time being I was at last safe with the space that I so desperately needed to start putting right what had gone wrong.

I had been with the community a few weeks and it was frustrating, things were not moving on as fast as I had hoped and it all started to feel like I was a prisoner in a pleasant setting, although it was pointed out to me by the Priest that I was far from being a prisoner as I could walk out the gate at anytime with no guard to stop me. The community was open for all who had been through a life crisis and worked on an ethic of work, rest and play. Everyone did work duties according to what they felt they could cope with but I could see it gave everyone a true sense of belonging and camaraderie. As great as it all was I felt myself going downhill, depressed and disinterested with all around me. It was a Thursday as far as I can remember; I hadn't slept properly for weeks. Easter had passed and we were into late April. The sun was shining and the usual buzz of the community was all around me. It had been a particularly tough few days, I had received threatening phone calls via my mobile phone, and how these people who were putting me through hell got the number I will never know. Due to my lack of sleep I had gone to see the doctor who prescribed some sleeping tablets. Sitting on a bench outside some cloisters with a cup of tea I tried to relax, my head was thumping and inside myself I was cracking up having endured over a year of fear, running and worry. It would be easy to just say I overdosed but that would not be true, I just wanted to sleep and for the pain I had felt all these months to just go away. Then darkness fell.

Nothing was real, a snippet here, a voice there. A shard of light and more voices "Jason can you hear me?" Am I dead? My voice croaked, swallowing my throat felt as if I had just eaten a thousand needles. The light was now blinding and I fought hard against it to get back to the limbo where I could be alone. The voices were now very loud and hard edges where taking shape all around me, then a face was visible looking down at me shining a torch into my eyes. A voice to the side of me said "You're ok; you're in hospital, you have been very lucky." My eyes were now clear and I could see two nurses and a doctor being busy around me. One of the community members sat next to me. Through a ragged throat that sounded more like finger nails being drawn down a blackboard I groaned "I've really blown it this time" my eyes closed and a merciful sleep took me.

Before being released from A&E a doctor came to talk to me, having heard only part of what drove me to such a low depth he said something that I had needed to hear for a long time, being if I killed myself those who would see me harmed would have won, at the very least I was doing them a favour, and they were obviously terrified of me, or what I knew or why else would they have tried to kill me, it made sense and was encouraged to talk with the authorities.

Going back to the community was quite hard after my ordeal, thinking I would be a laughing stock. It didn't happen that way, everyone just accepted what had happened, asked how I was and then got on with what they were doing. I was amazed and felt humbled and strangely accepted, not at all what was expected. The priest in charge took me to see a psychiatrist who having been told everything up to my recent hospital visit said that anyone under the circumstances I had been through would certainly have done the same and was pretty amazed how much I had endured before getting into the state that I had been in. It was now time to try and rebuild – start again from scratch. How this process was going to happen was uncertain.

It starts with breakfast

Community life is not easy, you have to learn to work and live with everyone in all situations. Living with London City Mission had already given me a good start but with a larger community comes greater responsibility to others and the surroundings you work in which is also your home. I had reconciled myself to my past and in part was moving on. I finally gave a statement to the police about all that had happened. No charge was brought against me and while everything was being investigated I was to stay with the community. This was part of the reason I was not settling in so well. Inwardly I felt exonerated and was desperate to get on with life, but spending so much time on the run and homeless looking over my shoulder had taken its toll. I knew it was wise to stay until all was sorted and I had healed inside from the post trauma of past events but now there was not so much to worry about it was difficult to get into everyday life. Life was passing by and I didn't even notice.

One morning after my usual late start the back door opened and in walked a member of the community, our community had a visitor from a sister community who had recently come to visit to help. He looked at me threw over a pair of gloves and said "we are going to the allotment to plant seeds" No thanks, I replied and tossed the gloves back, gardening is not my thing. "It's not your thing now but it will be" said the man and threw the gloves back while opening the door and walking down the path leaving me speechless!

Stomping behind my new co-worker I could hardly believe what had just happened, furious wouldn't describe just how mad I felt at that moment. He didn't say another word as we walked the path up to the allotment. We continued in silence in our planting of vegetable seeds with only the sound of the breeze on nearby trees and the odd groan coming from my direction. An hour or so passed and in that time, other than inwardly moan I began to wonder what motivated this man who was planting seed at a phenomenal rate, he surely can't be enjoying himself I thought. The bell at the main house rang it was time for a tea-break. While sipping tea I had to ask "Just how do you do this day in, day out?" I further explained my frustration of what felt like forever waiting and how it affected me and my lack of enthusiasm here at the community. The man took his time to answer; he finished his tea first and then rolled himself a cigarette. Just as It looked as though my question was going to be greeted with silence he replied "it's about losing your routine and discovering it again, what you need to do is start with breakfast. From there you have a daily foundation – a starting point where everything else can follow, after all your day needs to start somewhere" As much as I wanted to tell this man he was wrong, I couldn't. He had hit the nail on the head. It was from this point that recognisably I turned a corner. The next few weeks were tough having to get up at seven in the morning and over cornflakes and toast organise my day, but it worked and the community was suddenly not just a place where I had to live but my home and as I became more centred my confidence started to return opening new opportunities as I got stuck into daily work, cooking, building, my new friendships and funnily enough a passion for the garden!

The end of the beginning

Coming down for breakfast one morning I was in a contemplative mood. We had recently raised a barn and there was now another shed to be erected that was possibly large enough to become an art studio. Walking into the dining room I was met by one of the community helpers who excitedly told me I had received a parcel. Thing was I didn't get very much mail and having checked the post mark I never got mail from France. The helper told me she found it a little odd as the parcel was left by the main gate, even though the gate was opened and all post was delivered to the main house. Looking closely at the package it wasn't very well wrapped and had an oily stain at the top of it. Feeling very sick I told the community helper that we needed to make a phone call.

When I had given my statement to the police a few months back they felt it necessary to give me an event number and I was told in any unusual event to call them and quote the number given. I had hoped that this would never have to happen however a day or so before bombs had gone off in London and I was afraid the package was not what it seemed. To make matters worse the priest in charge and his wife had gone away for a few days so there was no one I could go to for help and the community volunteers were anxious for me to make the call. Within fifteen minutes the police arrived and evacuated the community to a residential home down the road. The roads around the old monastery were closed off and the army bomb disposal was called in. The police were great, as were the army and when we discovered a member of the community had gone off to find a phone box to call the press the officer in charge had it put out that the situation had been a false call. The parcel was found to be non threatening; some French company had randomly sent a model train to me? How this happened we will never know but it was enough for some intelligence unit to arrive at the community a few hours later to interview me. The officers put my mind at rest and I was left with instruction that I might have to be moved if they felt it necessary which I am pleased to say never happened. I thought I would be asked to leave the community but they were very understanding and in a way took a real risk with me of which I will be ever grateful for. The community really had become my family and expressed this with the highest compliment they could give. "Trust"

I continued to stay and work with the community until the middle of the following January. When it was time to say goodbye it was very sad. They had seen me through one of the darkest periods of my life, without question, blame or judgement. The morning I left I again smelt the strong aroma of that plant by the front door that had first greeted me on my arrival. One day I will smell that aroma again. The nightmare was over. I am a blessed man that I came out the other end of such events more or less intact. There would be further investigations into what had happened but this was not to include me. I had said all I could have said to the authorities and in the end it had been proved that I was unwittingly a victim of mistaken identity. You would think anger should have driven me to sue having been found innocent, however in the months of struggle fear and hardship leading up to this point I realised that some things are best left. Sometimes events are not in our control. I found myself thanking God that I live in a country where the authorities still care enough to follow through with their investigations and what had happened was a good part my own fault. Looking at things rationally had I not run in the first place I now believe the consequence of what happened would not have been so severe. I left the community that day a free man with my shoulders back and my head held high.

New beginnings

Having left the community with its allotment, fresh bread and wonderful scenery I found myself with a new job working on the coast. The job was horrible and although described as a Christian organisation it was far from it. However God moves in mysterious ways. While there I met two South Koreans on a year out from their studies. We soon became good friends and I enjoyed working with them. They introduced me to their culture and food and I soon became a big fan of Kim chi (a hot sauce with cabbage). I think my new friends could see how frustrated I was with this new job of mine, I really didn't fit it and I started to wonder if I had made a huge mistake by leaving the community. One particular bad day when all I seemed to do was make beds and wash up the Korean girl of the two asked how I would feel about going to Korea to teach English? To be frank this had never crossed my mind before but it caught my attention. She gave me a book on Korea to read and left me to my thoughts.

I consumed the book within a few hours sucking in all the information on the country and marvelling at the beautiful photographs. Long before I had finished reading I decided that this was the place to go. The next day I rang the authorities and asked if it would be possible to leave the country? The answer was positive telling me I was not needed as everything that happened would take some time to investigate and being that I had done nothing wrong I was encouraged to get on with my life as they would contact me when appropriate.

Four weeks later I found myself at Heathrow airport excitedly awaiting my flight to Seoul South Korea. It didn't feel sad to be leaving the U.K and I had no reservations with my decision apart from missing the new season of Doctor Who with this new guy called David Tennant that looked really good – still I thought to myself as my plane was called to board, there will always be DVD.

**South then North**

It was mid April and the sun was shining. Having sat on a plane for fourteen hours I walked stiffly towards arrivals and passport control at Incheon airport. My first glimpse of Korea had been as we came through the clouds to land to be met with high rise building glinting in the sunshine. Once through passport control and having collected my bags I made my way out to the bustling arrivals gate where there stood a heavily pregnant Korean lady holding a plaque with my name on. Having met my guide from the school I was to work at I was bundled into a waiting taxi and we sped toward a sub city outside of Seoul known as Suwon. Three things became very apparent that afternoon as we headed down the motorway. The first was that most Koreans adopted a western name; my guide introduced herself as Jane. The second was that the majority of Korean citizens lived in high rise buildings, I had read this in the book given me by my Korean friend in the U.K, but to see high rise buildings everywhere with your own eyes was really incredible as it showed the ingenuity of the Korean builders and engineers who utilised all available space. Thirdly it was clear by the speed we were going and the way other traffic were acting, not to mention I felt I was on a white knuckle ride, that the Koreans had no problem re enacting the Grand Prix! We arrived in Suwon (alive) and I was informed that the school wished to take me out to dinner that evening, guess they had never heard of jet lag, and I would be picked up from my new apartment. On entry my apartment looked Spartan yet comfortable, no bed? No problem there was a fold out futon or "kumo", which I later learned meant floating cloud and was of Japanese design. In the hour I had spare I felt a shower would be appropriate which took about forty five minutes due to the instructions being in Korean and the diagrams attaches were equally confusing. Still I won in the end and finished dressing just as my dinner benefactors arrived. Off we went a block down the road to a restaurant known as a Galbi house. No chairs but low cushions on the floor around a table with what looked like a barbeque in the middle where pork sizzled and smelt as good as it tasted. My legs had long gone to sleep by the time we had finished and my new Korean colleagues were amused as I tried to prize myself off the floor. Still all in all it was a positive start to my new career as an English teacher and the Korean contingent were very pleasant. I arrived back at my apartment having had no sleep for over twenty four hours; I barely rolled out the futon as I crashed fully clothed into a heavenly sleep.

## School

My new school, like many others in Korea, was clean and bright. The lessons would start at 9am and finish at 2pm working with kindergarten (primary) then a chance for a little rest and then from 5pm until 9pm I would teach high school kids. The lessons would be ordered by the school bell, unlike our western bell though this sounded like the ice cream van I remembered from my childhood, the first few days you go insane and go completely off wanting a Mr.Softee soft scoop but thankfully after a week or so it becomes a back ground noise and I am glad to write that a few weeks into school I rekindled my love affair with ice cream! The kids worked hard as their parents expected it and to begin with I hardly got to know my classes as they were studying so hard we had little time to talk. A few weeks into the semester though we all relaxed and managed to make up time even sharing the odd joke. It was during these more relaxed moments when I first started to learn about South Korea's desire to one day see reunification with their sister country North Korea. From the children, teachers and new friends I was making daily I heard stories of the North, learnt of the North South conflict in the 1950's and began to understand a country that in it's history had been separated by war and invasion for many years. I found the South Koreans a peaceful people with a rich culture whose country had only just got on its feet in the last thirty years, a country I was fast falling in love with.

A new challenge

Over 26% of Koreans are Christians. It was encouraging to see the churches over flowing and I found myself in a church within a high rise. The church was connected to a school that I had become friendly with since arriving in the country a month before. My faith and belief in God was still very flat after the events that had happened in the UK. I was happy to sit at the back and be the token westerner, besides I rarely understood the service apart from the odd phrase and some choruses sang, albeit in Korean with me singing the words in English. Unlike the regular English Sunday service the Korean version could go on for three hours plus but the people attending clearly enjoyed it which at the time made me feel a little ashamed of my lack of faith and how, even when on fire for God I could only handle an hour and a half of church at one time. On saying this I still didn't feel challenged and I guess this was transparent when the pastor came to chat with me. He was totally on fire for his belief and an encourager if I ever met one. Through this pastor I was introduced to a group of individuals who were interested in taking the Gospel into North Korea.

North Korea remains today, even as I write this, the last stronghold and bastion of solid Communism, it's cruel and unjust leaders have put their people into virtual slavery paling into significance any other communist regime. The bamboo curtain divides South and North, each side taking up positions since the end of hostilities in July 1953, although there has never been an official ceasefire. If you go to the DMZ (de militarized zone) there is a border line with a South & North Korean soldier standing nose to nose for hours on end. On the North side, so I was told behind military positions are waiting North Korean troops waiting for the order to invade or snatch any unwary person who should stray too close to their side of the border. To finish this ensemble of death the border land is one great mine field. To get into North Korea you have two routes, by plane to China and then across the border or the newly opened (in the last few years) diamond mountain pass, a border road with the south, one road in, one road out.

Having met with this group of people I was presented with one question "You have a British passport – good, North Koreans prefer British to American, so then how would you like a trip into the North?"

**Going North**

What had been asked of me was unexpected. It's one thing to go to another country to work but to be asked to do something a little crazy just wasn't the right thing to do – sorry only kidding, it was an adventure, I jumped at the chance. Making the decision to go was not without consequences. I had to leave my school to go to another in Deagu. Then I had to go back to the UK for three weeks while my papers were being organised, this proved to work well as it gave me time to visit the community I still missed.

Four weeks after agreeing to enter the north I found myself back at Incheon airport, this time there was no culture shock and no guide to pick me up on arrival, instead I was to catch an inbound flight to Deagu where I was told I would be collected. As my flight touched down in Deagu I felt a rush of excitement and fear. Getting through the arrival barrier in record time I was met and driven to a downtown motel and told my apartment would be ready to move into within two days, meanwhile relax. Chilling out was the last thing I could do feeling so keyed up so I skipped town to Suwon to meet up with friends for the weekend. On my return as promised was an apartment waiting for me. I started my new school the next day, which was more or less the same as the old one, just a bit smaller. All I could think about as I taught for the next three weeks was how it was going to work with my going into North Korea. It was a very long three weeks.

Sitting on the bullet train heading toward Seoul central it came upon me all of a sudden that this was for real and I wondered if I had made the right decision, too late now I argued to myself we had arrived at the station. A short trip on the underground and I found myself on a coach heading north.

If you look at a map Korea, both north and south, looks such a small country. Try telling the bus that. We seemed to go on forever making short stops at roadside garages that had seen better days, I will never complain about Welcome Break service stations again early the next morning we arrived at the border.

Passport control was interesting; on the south side I had to surrender my passport to be scrutinized for ten minutes while a throng of tourists chatted excitedly around me. Having my passport duly returned we again boarded our waiting bus to have our passports taken from us again to be given to the border guards to check. Then off the coach again as it was checked for goodness knows what but thoroughly as we were made to wait an hour. Eventually we arrived at what looked, at first sight, like a circus big top. As we neared the entrance and the view became clearer it looked shabby and needing some attention. Outside the entrance was a person dressed in an equally shabby bear suit, according to those I was travelling with it was to make us feel calm and welcome, to me it looked more like Tim Burton had done a makeover on Disney, it really was appalling and would have frightened any child under ten half to death. As Mr. Bear waved, I joined the queue waiting to enter in waving cheerfully back trying not to think that in some bizarre way I was bear baiting!

The inner tent was a shabby as the outer and very sparse. Here you had your identification checked again and then any hand luggage searched. Having gone through this charade you then had to walk through an x – ray machine and finally before you can walk through the door at the bottom of the corridor into North Korea you were asked to surrender any video equipment you were carrying including mobile phones, then told you would get them back on your return. I made my way down the corridor and out through the door, which at the time I thought odd as it was a wooden door in a tent, which led me to my waiting bus and a short drive to the tourists compound.

The North Koreans clearly wanted Western visitors to see only what they thought would help us believe North Korea was an up and coming power. The area we were taken too had been designed to give a false impression. On site there were two or three hotels, where I had to stay for two nights could have been a swanky London hotel complete with restaurant, bar and in house evening entertainment from a Philippine trio, who were pretty good. There was always a military presence who kept watch at all times that no – one went beyond the perimeter fence. If you did there would be a blowing of whistles and you were escorted back to the safety of the hotel zone for your own sake, that is what you are told and judging by the look on the faces of some of the soldiers I have no doubt they were telling the truth. In my opinion it was all a very pretty open prison camp.

The next two days we were driven around areas that had been pre-prepared for visiting. On admission the scenery we were shown was beautiful and often quite breath taking but I felt frustrated in not being able to speak with any North Koreans, the people we met were mainly military personnel or blue shirted guides who proudly wore a badge of office sporting the picture of their great and glorious leader Kim Jong IL that smiled at you no matter what angle you looked at it. The only working people we came across had to immediately sit down, some with hands on head as we were not authorized to see them work, we were also told we could not talk or have any contact with these poor wretches who eyes looked at the ground, any attempt to look up would be met with shouts from whatever authority there was nearby. So much for the freedom of communism! As we walked around and around the diamond mountains I managed to talk to one of the group who was seen as a veteran, he had visited the north four times. He understood my frustrations and assured me we were here for a higher purpose and to be patient. It was suggested that I took this time as a form of reconnaissance as all was never as it seemed. Settled for the moment I headed toward another ravine and bridge over a gorge. The mountains were still, not even a light breeze, as if they were themselves awaiting freedom.

On the second evening I met with the two others who had travelled with me. We had all been on different buses as it was felt that it were safer not to be seen together all the time. Both my counterparts had North Korean experience. I had been told on entry to this organisation that because of security and safety most people involved have a shelf life of six visits into the north this particular way. After that the authorities tend to grow suspicious of why you love visiting so much that could lead to awkward situations. On saying this there are many people who either visit the north or are able to stay officially who daily put their lives on the line by getting Bibles and supplies to the underground church. It all felt a little like a spy film as people were met and certain phrases were used to identify who we and they were. There was a brief handover with no conversation. That was it, no big drama, no sirens blasting through the night with soldiers running over to capture us, just stars and moon looking down on us as we made our way back to our hotels for a drink and then bed.

**Five more times then**

The first couple of trips into the north were pretty much the same as the first. On my return from each trip I would continue to teach South Korean children and students their vowels and mark essays sometimes having to completely re-write them for the pupil to have to rewrite the next time I saw them. It all seemed very easy. Things started to change though from the fourth time I ventured over the border. The north was / is happy to receive professional help especially in the area of medicine, as long as it is free. Two European medical graduates were desperate for an adventure over the border so off we went. We were allowed to go beyond the western compound into the rural areas. Rural would be a bad description as we trundled over little more than mud tracks to small townships. The people had nothing, and I mean nothing. Then again they had nothing to complain about because they knew nothing more as they were educated to believe everyone was in the same boat. The houses were nothing but basic that sometimes resembled wattle and daub. Food was always scarce and people walked around and worked daily on the brink of starvation. Funnily enough I never met an overweight North Korean civilian or soldier. I say soldier loosely as the way they looked depended on rank. Yes the common soldier was better fed and you could argue that their weight was due to the intense training programme all the troops have to undertake. However once you get to the more senior ranks you see a remarkable difference in size, so would that be down to less training or more food then? The country's leaders fare even better than the military's senior officers. A whole country of people having to starve while being fed the lie that it's for the benefit of their country, oh yes and it's the West's fault because we are nothing but fat capitalists who won't share with our communist's neighbours. Meanwhile the top 2% live in their ivory towers eating western food, wearing western suits, smoking cigars and drinking expensive whisky. Sadly there would be no point in telling these very lovely people we were working with the truth. They just wouldn't be able to understand what we were telling, if they believed us at all. The only people who believed different were the underground church; more because they had come to faith and having done so realised they had been lied to making it twice as dangerous for them. The North Korean government see them as a threat not just because they spread the gospel which in turn dispels communism, but also they see Kim Jong IL as a god to be worshipped – sorry correction that's how he likes to see himself and believes all people should do the same. So we would go into these villages and towns, the good doctors would minister what medical aid they could, and were allowed, while I played the pack horse carrying boxes and trying to help as much as possible. It was often not the best organised team but we got things done and tried to be the best witness we could.

We were always viewed with suspicion. It was hard work, our Korean guides would not speak with us as they believe, or had been taught to think, that no westerner could speak the Korean language and even though we had all picked up various words in Korean we kept our mouths shut and only spoke in English when we had to or thought in necessary as we were sure that our guides could understand English very well and had been put with us to report our movements and conversations – just as well that we believe that anyone can learn English or I guess our guides would have been in real trouble!

We got as much material to the underground church as we could. It was often difficult because of the danger it could put the receivers in. The underground church live in fear for their lives daily. If they are caught more often than not, scratch that – every time a church member is caught they are incarcerated by the authorities. When they are not convinced to turn away from their faith and embrace Kim Jong IL's leadership as total they are either imprisoned in some gulag which would no doubt mean death or executed immediately. Executions are normally performed in front of the townspeople or village folk where the prisoner comes from. This is to further suppress any more "Faith Meetings" in the area. The condemned are normally sentenced to death on the excuse of treason, or some other trumped up charge. They are then killed horribly without mercy; many are lined up flat down on their faces and driven over by steam roller, shot or crucified in arctic conditions on gulag walls. Many are beaten and tortured beforehand. Their crime? To openly believe talk and pray

**showing that Jesus Christ is their Lord and Saviour. Yet amazingly more people turn to Christ every day. North Korea really is seeing revival through persecution. Christians will walk miles to fellowship, worship and encourage one another knowing the danger but seeing the reward of heaven as a better proposition.**

**An excerpt from a report:**

### North Korea trying to expose underground church

A disconcerting report is coming out of a fairly reliable North Korea watchdog source, reports MNN.

According to the report, the North Korean government is reportedly setting up fake underground churches and disguising national security agents as defectors to expose Christians.

Voice of the Martyrs Canada's Glenn Penner can't confirm specifics. However, based on the source, he says, "Apparently, they're going into China, infiltrating the Korean churches that are assisting the North Korean defectors, and then coming back into North Korea with money and with Bibles, with the whole idea of unmasking Christians and also taking the funds and then using them for the North Korean government."

Penner says it's not a totally new strategy. He notes the Soviets did something similar during the Cold War, but he urges prayer. "Continue to pray for wisdom and for discernment on the part of believers who work in such restrictive nations. There's always the fear of discovery. You don't want to be controlled by fear, and these are really good prayers to be praying for our brothers and sisters, that the Lord would rule, and not fear."

North Korea has been described as one of the most repressive and isolated nations in the world. The nation is governed under a state religion called "Juche," meaning "self-reliance."

According to VOMC, citizens are required to worship their dead leader, the "Eternal President" Kim Il Sung, and his son, the current dictator Kim Jong IL.

Churches have been bulldozed, and Christians must practice their faith in secrecy and constant danger. Religious prisoners are often subjected to harsher treatment and given the most dangerous tasks, all in an effort to force them to renounce their faith. When they refuse, they have often been tortured to death.

**Recently after a church service, in which I led the prayers, here in the U.K I got challenged by a Christian who asked "why did you only pray for the underground churches in Korea and China?" I explained that as an example in Pyongyang there are three state churches. These churches have been set up by the government. They spy for the government while receiving gift aid from churches outside of North Korea. They infiltrate both the**

underground churches in N.Korea and China with one goal in mind – the destruction of the true Christians who have to meet in fear because of their governments and how they are treated if they are caught. They accept bibles on behalf of Christians in N.Korea which end up being incinerated. This is why I couldn't pray for the churches in N.Korea and China. My point is we need to be specific in what we pray for and what we say so there can be no misunderstanding in what is happening. Our brothers and sisters are living in persecution. Let's at least try, as Christians who are not under a tyrannical persecution, and get it right for them.

My own faith was flimsy at best and then I learnt and realised what was happening to the Christians here in North Korea. That day was like a sledge hammer hitting me full in the chest, like my heart had been shocked back into life. I had been sleeping far too long putting my faith over the years again and again in man and not my God. North Korean Christians pray daily for the West to become spirit filled and for revival. Humbling to say, they don't pray for themselves, other than numbers will increase and many will be saved through Christ and the same for the western Churches. Coming to this knowledge how could I continue the way I was? Limp, luke warm and inward looking. Was I ever saved in the beginning all those years ago? No doubt I could probably write pages in arguments for and against such a conclusion; however this is not what this about. It would be the right thing to say though that I felt re-born again, if that's not too confusing?

Everything felt crystal clear. It didn't matter how bad my past was, how as a child I had suffered a crippling and humiliating illness. It didn't matter that I screwed up after my divorce or the inner pain, conflict and anger I had felt. No longer did it matter that I again turned from God and the disasters I found myself in because of my own stupidity. It was time for me to stop beating myself up and taking all the blame upon my shoulders. At the moment when I had this epiphany I came to realise my struggles and walk with Christ was not just about Jason de-Vaux Balbirnie and in the great scheme of things I and all I had been through was insignificant.

### Tinker, tailor, Soldier Christian spy

I had now been in and out over the border a good few times. It all felt a bit pressurized knowing that you are trying to do the right thing but realizing that it couldn't go on forever, the North Koreans are far from stupid and we knew our usefulness was coming to an end aware that our every move was being monitored making it harder to take in supplies and materials without being caught. It was decided that as a team we would do one last trip and do as much as we could in the two days we would have. All went well in preparation including the paperwork we needed for the trip. On arrival the work continued as usual, the doctors doing their thing, me running behind trying for the life of me to look efficient and medical like. We got all our supplies out within the first day and in doing so relaxed a little. It was late summer and the leaves were starting to change colour with the air becoming marginally cooler, fall / autumn was just around the corner. The summer had been very hot, as usual. North Korea does not have the luxury of medicines like we do in the west, well the ordinary working folk don't. A Scarlet Fever epidemic had started, the city folk were faring better as were the countries leadership and high level military officers, no surprises there, but the rural folk suffered in their droves.

It was the second day and we happily slapped one another on the back for a job well done. Heading back toward the border we discussed our plans for the future and where we might be within the next year. Our guides were unusually quiet that day, I figured they must have fallen out, communist or not they were still human and although they tried to show no emotion or weakness in front of us you can always feel tension when people argue or disagree. We pulled into a rough field area for a comfort break; as usual I was the last back to the vehicle. On arrival my two companions looked a little worried and explained that our guides had been radioed and were to take us back up the track a few kilometres to a small township we had recently passed. I wouldn't have thought twice about it except for the look on the two faces that had greeted me. We sat in silence not knowing what to say to each other and fearing the worst for the short journey. As we arrived there were two military Lorries waiting and a handful of N.Korean soldiers. This at first didn't worry us as a military presence was always visible no matter where you were in the north. Our vehicle parked up and one of our blue shirted guides made their way over to the parked Lorries and pointed over in our general direction. Then the guide returned with two of the soldiers. We were asked for our papers which we promptly produced as they were always attached to lanyards around our neck with our photo I.D pointing forward at all times. It was then that I felt scared as one of the soldiers put the I.D's given into a bag. Our guide explained that we were to go with the soldiers and trucks for our own protection. Having walked over to the trucks we were then told by our guide that we would be taken to the border, but before we left the government would like us to give a short written statement to say why we were currently in North Korea. One of my colleagues protested and asked for our paperwork back. With that a soldier came forward and started to raise his voice, he was the officer in charge. Our guide explained, as the officer shouted, that it was thought that we had come to his country to cause disharmony among the people and to incite them to rise up against Kim Jong IL. It was then asked could we prove otherwise and if we couldn't then we would have to go with him to be further questioned. Then the officer pointed and said C.I.A!

It didn't seem to matter that our papers were in order, nor the fact that they had been taken and not returned. We sat in the back of the lorry. My stomach hurt and all I could think of was the ending of film the Great Escape, I explained this to my comrades who felt it inappropriate to be discussing such a film at this moment, we should be praying and didn't I realise that the prisoners had been shot at the end of the film? And it just wasn't funny! This was mad, how can they accuse us of being American spies, Bible smugglers yes but not spies, this was all very surreal and we hoped we would at least be taken to some government official who would be sensible about this. We seemed to drive forever. N.Korea is not a massive country and I started to worry that we were being driven around until nightfall to be shot under the cover of darkness – then again – no this is not possible as they could kill us any time they wanted. There was plenty of times they could have stopped in the middle of nowhere, "No" I thought, "let's be positive about this." Then the lorry stopped and we were told to get out.

We were back in the Western compound. I wasn't sure if I should laugh or wet myself. Our bags were unceremoniously dumped at our feet. The officer said something to his men which was obviously funny because they all fell about laughing like possessed pantomime dames. Then there was an order delivered and they all went rigid again? Our captor told us in very bad English that we were lucky, it seemed our story had been checked. So did they drive us around on a tour of fear just to make us squirm? It's the only answer we could fathom. From the compound we were taken back to the border. Before we took our leave we were told we could never return to the North and if we did the penalty would be severe. It had been a crazy twenty four hours and although tired and dirty as I arrived back in South Korea I felt like I had won the lottery, it was good to be alive.

A day or so later having had the luxury of a shower, sleep within clean sheets and fresh clothing I was sitting at a bar watching the CNN news. My attention was suddenly grabbed with a story of how a North Korean missile narrowly missed the coast of Japan. The international community were a little outraged by this show of what was seen as North Korea waving its war sabre. Although the North was saying it was an accident the United Nations decided that it would impose economic sanctions. This had all happened while I was still in the North a few days previously. I couldn't but help wonder if this dramatic turn of events had in some way been part of the outcome in recent days? It was later discovered through an anonymous contact that due to the sanctions imposed there was little medication to treat the Scarlet fever epidemic that I and others had witnessed. Sadly the result was that many died and even sadder, the events of this disaster were never reported on by the media. As the news story came to an end I had to leave. I am not sure if it was the surge of guilt and anger I was feeling or that I was trying to avoid anyone seeing the tears running down my face.

Sadly I don't think I will ever get back into North Korea again, unless that there is a shift in power and reunification happens in my life time, which I pray it will. It was sad to say goodbye to my two friends, who felt they should now take their skills somewhere else, they were off to some African state and I wondered as I waved them off if they will ever have enough of the life they lead? They really have a special ministry and part of me wanted to follow them but we knew our paths had to part at this junction in our walks. I feel humbled and blessed for the experiences that have remoulded me.

## Songs of the South

Deagu rail station is always busy, next door there is a Lotte department store, people hurry by trying to catch a train or rush by you with carrier bags full of clothes and goods as they head to the nearby taxi rank to ferry them to whatever apartment block they live in. Many times I have sat at the top of the escalators watching; wondering what would happen if there was a sudden emergency or crisis. Would the people below just continue anyway? Locked in their own worlds unaware of either their surrounding or the people they pass. Scattered around are what looks like old heaps of rag and paper, if you looked closer you realise the piles are human beings, more scarecrow then people. At closer inspection it's surprising to find that the highest percentage of these South Korean homeless are either well over sixty, disabled or both. These are the people who have no one to look after them; unlike the U.K there are no real services to help and so they have to fend for themselves begging or selling small items that have been found here and there. One man comes to mind who I would see on the subway rolling up and down the carriages on a board with wheels, he had no legs. A fellow traveller explained to me when I had first arrived that he was no doubt a war veteran with no family to support him, it was truly awful to witness and for good or bad you couldn't but help give the poor man a few thousand Won to try and help him. These people are generally ignored by the trendy youth and those coming and going to work, all MP3's and the latest mobile, it astounded me how little time people had for these old and infirm people.

I saw her every time I walked down the steps to the subway, hand raised up and palm out hoping for a little money. To my shame I had walked past many times almost without thought. She was very old and the etching lines on her face told a story of hardship. Her skin was tight around her face showing how under nourished she was. Not long after my return from the border I again passed this woman, stooped over because of age taking the rejection of those who passed by quietly almost as if she was resigned to her fate. As I passed she caught my eye, without saying a word I could see she was in desperate need, she looked thinner than usual and at the point of collapse. By now she had sat down on the concrete. I couldn't pass and leave her. I reached down and stuffed some notes into her hand. Something more than words passed from her to me as she sat in disbelief. Holding my sleeve she just kept saying thank you in Korean with tears in her eyes. As I walked on it came to me that I hadn't just helped a stranger in need but in the moment I had just shared I had gained a grandmother. With this in mind I went back to find her but when I had reached the spot where she had been it was empty. It couldn't have been any more than five minutes since we parted and realising how old she was figured she was sure not to be far away. I ran back up the steps toward the station, there was no sign of her. Before leaving Korea I went back a few times but never encountered the woman again. Who she was I will never know but what she taught me at that day was an awareness and responsibility for all in the world who need more than love or money – they need family.

My last "wild" experience was on a bus journey from the satellite town I lived in. Korean buses are always packed and more often than not you get standing room only, especially on the bus to down town Deagu. The bus driver was yet another formula one fan as the bus hurtled down the highway. I was standing up hanging on for dear life. Looking down the bus there was a man that looked at a guess in his seventies. Being the only westerner on the bus might have accounted for his staring at me, but westerners are common place in South Korea what with American airbases and the hundreds of ex pats who go out to teach English every year. Turning my attention to look out the window I hoped his staring was in my imagination, or had I offended him somehow? On looking back he was still staring, no blinking just looking ahead toward me. The next thing that happened I was unprepared for and really weirded me out. The man / or something that resembled the man left his body and flew up to my face. The look on what only can be described as this ghoulish figures face was truly the ugliest thing I had ever seen. It flew up to me, looked me up and down and then returned to the body of the man still staring. A few moments later the bus stopped. The man offered me his seat, although there were many people standing who had been on the bus longer than me. As he passed me to get off he apologised that he had been so rude with no control. Shocked I let him past. Having thought this event through many times I have concluded it was definitely a spiritual encounter. Whatever had come from the man couldn't or wouldn't touch me, I have to believe it was because God protected me, it can be the only sensible conclusion I can come up with and proved to me that as Christians we should always be prepared to come up against the unbelievable and be ready for spiritual warfare in any given situation.

A kind of homecoming

*How do you pick up the threads of an old life? How do you go on, when in your heart you begin to understand, there is no going back. There are some things that time cannot mend. Some hurts that go too deep.*

**Frodo Baggins: *The Lord of the rings.***
            ***The return of the king.***

On landing, Heathrow airport was very cold. I had been cold in Korea but the weather there was starting to change and although any local Korean would tell you it was still cold the day I left warm air was caressing the earth and mountains, to me it had felt like Spring. It was late evening as I strolled out of the airport doors to look for a cab. Icy gusts of wind hit my face as I made my way to the taxi rank. All around me was night illuminated by the airport and surrounding street lights. Glad to find a waiting cab I slung my rucksack in the back and hurriedly jumped into the passenger seat out of the cold. I had the foresight to book a room at a nearby hotel knowing I would be arriving late into the country, in the morning I was to travel to the midlands to stay with friends while I decided what to do next. The short journey to my hotel gave me chance to catch my breath, it felt odd to be back in the U.K after all that had happened and I couldn't help but wonder if I should have taken one of the teaching job offers I had received to either stay for another year in Korea or accept the offer in China after a recent whistle stop tour there. I felt my eyes shutting, it had been a long journey back, via Hong Kong and I was glad when we arrived so I could bath and go to bed. It was months since I had slept in a European bed, I missed my futon and eventually had to take the mattress off the bed and put it on floor to get to sleep. Even now nearly three and half years down the road I still prefer a mattress on the floor to a bed.

It was all a little odd the next morning, finding my feet again I knew would be hard and as I made my way to the train station it was hard to concentrate with my surroundings looking and feeling so different. My train to the midlands was running late by forty five minutes and it was still freezing cold. The station in the late winter morning light looked depressing which didn't help with my frame of mind. Finally, after two trips to WH Smiths and a hot chocolate I forced myself onto the train telling myself everything would be all right. Within a couple of hours I was in Staffordshire in my new lodgings which were pleasant enough and it was good to catch up with old friends. Mercifully the day had passed swiftly enough and as I headed to my bed, or should that be mattress I started to take stock and think ahead about what I should do next.

Job hunting was a slow and almost painful task, it wasn't that I didn't want to work, and there just were no jobs. I didn't want to sign on and I had saved a little bit of money from teaching in South Korea which would sustain me for a while. I needed a distraction and it came in way of friends moving house in Bristol. Having been back in the U.K for three weeks I found myself on yet another train, this one on time, travelling south to paint walls. It was now March and thankfully the weather was finally changing. The sun was shining as I arrived at Temple Meads station and for the first time since being back in the country life felt a lot better. I spent the next five weeks painting and decorating and doing little else other than the odd trip back to Staffordshire for job interviews. My friends had been with me in the London City Mission days and over the years we had managed to stay in contact in one shape, form or another. The wife in the partnership was the sister of the girl I had fallen in love with all those years back but because of the four year age gap had banned us from going out together. Having gone out one morning to return a broken pressure washer on behalf of the house I returned to find the self same girl, now in her thirties, arriving for lunch with us. We had seen each other briefly before a few years previous at a fortieth birthday bash but here we were now making sandwiches and being able to talk properly for the first time in sixteen years. Having met a couple more times over a couple of weeks I realised that this time there was no big sister blocking our way – so I asked her out!

Four months later we were married.


Having been involved with Methodists in Korea I felt it right to nail my colours to the post and put myself under authority with this particular denomination. When I was a child I had been baptized Methodist, had Methodist on my wrist band while in hospital and attended a Methodist Sunday school. The Lord moves in mysterious ways and in a turn of events I felt He had brought me home, not just to the U.K but to a whole new beginning, a great Church a wife and a family, we were expecting a baby girl.

As I have been writing over these last months and read my notes and diary again and again I realise that there is a thread through my stories and testimony. The thread being the Lord, He has walked with me before I knew Him right up to now. This should come as no shock to a Christian of coming up to twenty five years but it is only when you start to write and put things into perspective that you begin to take on board the significance of your daily walk and relationship with the Almighty. My Christian experience might seem or come across as amazing or exciting to some. Please be assured it is / has been far from either. Most days since coming to the Lord I have wished that I came from a stable Christian background with none of what has happened. We are all different with our testimonies and personalities going into a vast melting pot that helps keep Christianity live, vibrant and unique. Therefore as much as I have wished and sometimes tried to run away from the path that God leads me to I have submitted to His will knowing that my

Heavenly Father only has what is best in my interests. It has been a long and sometimes painful road so far but after having wished I was someone else, ran away from God, arrested, imprisoned, accused, beaten, abused, called a liar, laughed at and faced death I have come to standstill in a cool and shady place where I have been able to lay my head and recover. To be re-born again and been blessed because our Father never sells us short and will always bring us home to safe harbour if we choose to walk with Him. With everything behind me and all in front to get excited about the bottom line is it's just good to just be – just to be Jason.

**Messages**

For those who don't yet know Jesus or who are seeking:

My friends, God is real and Jesus is alive. I can believe it is a struggle to acknowledge something that you can't physically see. You may feel that praying to Jesus and asking Him into your life makes you uncomfortable. You may have heard many things from different people, Christian and non believers alike and you feel confused or pressured. My testimony that you have read stands true and yes I have missed some things out and concentrated on what I feel led to be important. Don't let what man says to you dictate. If you feel ready to pray and ask Christ into your life I would encourage you to go ahead – it's the best thing you will ever do, but do it because you want to and not because someone tells you too. Whatever stage you are at or even if you have just read this book or been to church once or thinking what the heck is this guy talking about the bottom line is Jesus Christ, He loves you and always has, He knew you from your conception and birth and He knows you now. He knows how you feel and is standing waiting for you with His arms open. He died for you and all the stupid things you ever did or thought Jesus wiped them away that day on the cross. Want to know more? If you are already in a church situation or have Christian friends go find them, talk to someone you feel you can trust like the church minister and ask them to pray with you, you can still pray by yourself, and if you have great, but it's also good to pray with other people. If you don't have a church connection but you have read this book and you are curious to discover more there are loads of churches out there who would love to meet you, please don't worry, they don't bite and will not smother you. If you are unsure what is best for you or confused where to go to church please go to the contact information at the front of this book and use the internet link. My prayer is that whoever you are God will meet you this day. He doesn't mind who you are, your background, ethnicity, sexuality or gender, God loves you and if you are good enough for the Lord you most certainly are good enough for the church. If you have a bible check it out go to the New Testament, the bible is basically in two parts old and New Testament. What you are looking for is toward the back of the book in the Gospels Mathew, Mark, Luke & John. Ok its John you need to read John chapter 3 verse 16. Can't find it? No worries just check out the internet link at the front of this book. It's a good place to start your journey.

**To those who have fallen**

You know if you once walked amongst Christ's people, maybe you sometimes still do? The question is what went wrong? Whether you burnt out, decided it was all fiction or you simply walked because of personal reasons "COME BACK" you are important to Christ and you are loved. The day you fell there was mourning in Heaven and angels wept. God called you by name and is so doing again. If you really walked with the Lord you will feel daily the battle that rages within you, the knowledge that you knew the King of Heaven and now you have an empty hole within you that nothing you have tried has managed to fill. No doubt you have come across old friends from church, do you feel unsettled or embarrassed when they stop to say hello? Is it all too much? Do you feel you just want to be left alone? As already said people walk away from Christ and church for so many different reasons. It's your choice in how you act after reading this. I am sure you have heard many different and persuasive arguments from other people and within yourself. I can only tell you this, you are being prayed for, Christ will be coming back, please don't throw away your salvation because you have met someone you like who's not a Christian, you feel you have blown it because of one stupid act, your marriage broke up, you started to drink or do drugs, you felt the world had something better to offer, someone you loved died and you blame God, you are confused and you just don't know what to believe anymore – and many, many other reasons. Come back to your God, hear His call and feel His Spirit and anointing on your life once more – be revived. If you feel you can't do this alone for any reason I urge you to seek out one Christian you know of you can trust. Talk with that person and seek council. Please I beg you don't leave it any longer. Our Heavenly Father is calling your name; you have nothing to fear and nothing to lose.

Hebrews 3: 14

To the church

This is NOT just for the Methodist church. This is for all churches out there whatever denomination you stand behind.

How many brothers and sisters have we lost over the years? I am not talking about through death but those who have fallen from the path of the cross. Those who backslid from view, those we have pushed away because it was felt that they were spiritually unclean. Over the years we have seen many fall along the wayside – should we let this continue? I say NO. We have a duty to seek out our brethren who no longer walk with us, to stand with them and offer healing and where needed forgiveness, understanding and assurance. Let's not be so hasty to throw out the baby with the bath water. In no way am I trying to judge the church, I am no better than you, it's just that in the last few years, especially when I too found myself in the dark and on the streets I met many who had fallen, people who, like you and I knew Christ and witnessed the works of His Holy Spirit here on earth. There were many who had been in ministry and when a life crisis struck needed support and care but received none. The stories I have been witness too have come from far and wide, yes some might not be true or the whole truth but I would say to you there were many men and women who are now broken due to a harsh word, a judgement or falling out. I also came across those with mental instability who had been accused of being demon possessed when they needed a doctor, medicine and understanding, we are so quick to judge one another, beware my friends, think before you act. The blood of the many lost and fallen is on our hands. If you feel you have made the wrong judgement call or you know / knew of a situation go deal with it NOW, don't leave it to fester. Many years ago when I first come to the Lord the youth group I was involved with did a dance drama called "The battle" it spoke of two churches Holy Hill and the Broken City. Bottom line one of the main characters gets tempted and steals from Holy Hill, the people within that church can't see beyond their own arrogance and would be holiness and cast the man out; the Broken City accepts this man and heals him showing forgiveness. So which one are we? Holy Hill where we pay lip service and live to show the world how great we are – or do we dwell among the Broken City where we evangelise the unsaved who in turn can see that we are truly Gods people as they see us showing mercy to our people even when things have gone badly wrong. Come let us seek these lost brothers and sisters and bring them home.

Romans 8: 35 - 39

To the persecuted church

My brothers and sisters take heart, you are being prayed for day and night. We can't begin to comprehend what you go through because of your faith in Jesus Christ. We are not persecuted here in the West as you, we still have the freedom to meet publically without fear of arrest, charge or execution and what humbles us is that while you live at your peril you pray for us, that revival will come to the West and many will find the Lord. The day will come soon when you are no longer tethered by cruel masters and their power and governments will fall. If any of you dictators and cruel governments get to read this understand, Christ is coming to judge the living and the dead. You have slain our Father's people to fulfil your own greed and bloodlust, however there is still time, look at the people you persecute, remember those you have slain. Do you not realise that Jesus Christ died for all mankind —and yes this means you too? Ask forgiveness of the Lord, He will hear your plea and have mercy.

My friends, who are this day in fear of your life, have faith and know that your sufferings are not in vain. Your witness, your cries do not go unheard. Nothing is forgotten.

**2 Corinthians 4: 8 - 11**

**Peace be with you**

## Epilogue

May 2010. As this is being written there is once again warmth in the air, a bee buzzes past followed by a red admiral. It's all lovely and tranquil, almost perfect. As I look up into the blue sky and wonder why time goes by so quickly?

I got the job at Wesley Methodist Cambridge and it's nearly four months into the post. To have had the opportunity to reflect on the past and share testimony with anyone who cares to read what has been written is a privilege. It turns out God is so much bigger than we can ever imagine. He is with us past present and future. This book started as diaries of events that have changed and shaped me which I conclude will continue until my Lord calls me home. I have no idea what the future will bring but there is nothing to fear because Jesus is real and with Him by my side for what reason is there to worry?

The last twenty three years of my life have been incredible, crazy and educational. I can't change the past but I have a choice in what might happen tomorrow by the way I act today, yes there are times when sadness of past events momentarily overtake me, feelings of guilt. Questions of could I, should I, why did I but within everything said in no way would I ever try to remove myself from responsibility for any action or discretion. I have learnt so much from everything that has happened and I am grateful my faith rests in a compassionate and faithful God.

My friends be encouraged. Write your words of testimony and tell the world. There are millions of stories out there all different but each with a constant that is Jesus Christ. Remember that Christianities story didn't end with the book of Revelations it just got bigger!

My name is Jason de-Vaux Balbirnie. I am comfortable in my own skin, in whom and what I am. A servant who follows the King known as Jesus.

God be with us all in what is and has to come.

Printed in Great Britain
by Amazon.co.uk, Ltd.,
Marston Gate.